CLEAR LAKE PUBLIC LIBRARY

1 6102 00137 0481

The Historic Park Inn Hotel and City National Bank

720.9777 Haun, Katherine
HAU   Historic Park Inn
             Hotel and City National
             Bank

      1/11   29.95

k, Inc.

 Y0-BZK-595

PUBLIC LIBRARY
CLEAR LAKE, IOWA 50428

The missi...   ...serve, maintain and educate the
public ab...   ...ties across from Central Park in

1

DEMCO

WRIGHT ON THE PARK

The Historic Park Inn Hotel and City National Bank
Prepared for Wright on the Park, Inc.
Katherine Haun
Graduate Student in Historic Preservation, Ball State University
July 2007

Edited by Pat Schultz, Wright on the Park, Inc. Board of Directors, 2008-2010

Cover: Tinted period photographic postcard showing northeast perspective of the City National Bank and Park Inn Hotel Building, Mason City, Iowa. Collection of Wright on the Park, Inc.

Frontispiece: 1910 rendering of City National Bank and Park Inn Hotel Building, Mason City, Iowa, *Ausgeführte Bauten und Entwürfe von Frank Lloyd Wright*, Berlin: Wasmuth, 1911.

Drawings by Frank Lloyd Wright are copyrighted ©2010 Frank Lloyd Wright Foundation, Scottsdale, AZ.

FRANK LLOYD WRIGH ®
FOUNDATION
ASSOCIATE

Table of Contents

PUBLIC LIBRARY
CLEAR LAKE, IOWA 50428

Acknowledgements

The Historic Park Inn Hotel and City National Bank[i] was first drafted for Wright on the Park, Inc. (WOTP) in the summer of 2007 by Ball State intern Katherine Haun. The summer project was supported in part by a fellowship from the Keeper's Preservation Education Fund. The fellowship was established in 1988 by William J. Murtagh, the first Keeper of the National Register of Historic Places. It provides students, interns or established preservation professionals with funds to continue or support education.

The initial writing of this history would not have been possible without the help and advice from Terry Harrison and Arthur Fischbeck at the Lee P. Loomis Archives, Mason City Public Library, in Mason City, Iowa. Both men provided extensive knowledge of the social, political, and personal lives of major players in the development of the City National Bank and Park Inn Hotel. Without their assistance, the task of searching through the entire archive would have taken much longer.

Special thanks to Martha Huntington, AIA, and Dr. Robert McCoy, AIA (hon), for their patience in answering all questions concerning the Prairie School design and construction of the City National Bank and Park Inn Hotel.

Thanks must also be extended to the entire WOTP Board of Directors and Ann MacGregor, Executive Director. Without their support the summer project would never have been completed.

KH

Editing and updating of the history by Pat Schultz, WOTP Board of Directors, continued through 2008 into 2010 and was greatly assisted by WOTP Executive Director Ann MacGregor; board members Dr. Robert McCoy, Robert S. Kinsey III, Jean Marinos, and Peggy Bang; project architect Martha Huntington; and program assistant, Claudia Collier.

Special thanks also to Margo Stipe, Curator and Registrar of Collections for the Frank Lloyd Wright Foundation, for reviewing the manuscript and for her encouragement. Permission from the Frank Lloyd Wright Foundation to publish drawings and other materials is also greatly appreciated.

PS

---

[i] The title of this history reflects the name selected for the hotel in 2009, "The Historic Park Inn Hotel and City National Bank," which avoids conflicts with trademark restrictions on names and logos for other hotels. This name is used throughout the book in reference to the building and restoration as it exists today. However, historic references retain the name used in the specific time period. Thus the City National Bank and Park Inn Hotel is used when it was the name by which the building was known; the same is true for the Frank Lloyd Wright Apartments, etc., as they were then called and/or listed in city directories, phone books and other publications. When quoted material is used, the name remains the same as in the original source.

Overview

Frank Lloyd Wright designed The City National Bank and Hotel in his early architectural style called Prairie School. Commissioned through Mason City attorneys J.E.E. Markley and James E. Blythe, Wright created a modern bank, office and hotel for the prominent corner of State and Main (now Federal) Streets in the bustling city center.[1]

The bank proved a successful venture until the 1920s farm crisis. After a bankruptcy sale in 1926, new owners remodeled the bank building into commercial retail space, drastically altering its original design. The hotel, with few changes to its exterior, retained its function under various ownerships until 1972 and its conversion into apartments.

Included in Ernest Wasmuth's 1910-1911 Berlin publication *Ausgeführte Bauten und Entwürfe von Frank Lloyd Wright*, Wright's plans and drawings for the building drew immediate international attention. Locally, the style, characterized by wide overhangs, low proportions and use of natural building materials, set the tone for an explosion of Prairie School architecture in Mason City. Wright himself repeated many of its design elements in his famous Midway Gardens and Imperial Hotel. In Europe, Modernist architects used his principles in their own designs.

Today, The Historic Park Inn Hotel and City National Bank is the last standing example of Wright's five built hotels. The structure, which retains much of its original form, still serves as an excellent example of the Prairie School style. Wright on the Park, Inc., the local non-profit organization which now owns the building, is dedicated to the restoration-rehabilitation of this national treasure as well as its continued preservation in the future.

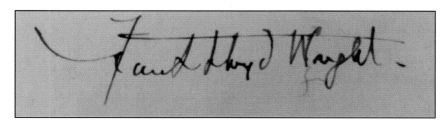

Wright's signature from a letter to Dr. Stockman, January 1, 1911, Lee P. Loomis Archives, Mason City Public Library, Mason City, Iowa.

[1.] Street names were changed to their current designation in 1916. State Street remained the same; however, Main Street became Federal Avenue.

City National Bank and Park Inn Hotel

In 1873, the City Bank was founded on the southeast corner of Main and State Streets by Thomas Emsley.[2] He was its first president. When he died, his wife Mary became president, continuing so for several years. In 1891 the bank incorporated, changing its name formally to the City National Bank with James Rule elected as the bank's first president under the new name. The success of the bank is evident in the amount of capital it held at its incorporation and ten years later, increasing from $50,000 to $100,000.[3]

At the turn of the century, Mason City was a growing community as a result of the booming farming market, successful brick and tile factories, and flourishing cement plants. The Chicago, Milwaukee and St. Paul Railroad expanded its line westward, making Mason City a major connecting point for four rail lines. With the commercial and industrial sectors established, the population of the city more than doubled between 1870 and 1890.[4] The era between 1910 and 1920 is often considered the "golden age of building construction" in Mason City. The population of the city again doubled in this golden age when industry was at its peak.[5] The economic boom of the area was favorable for a new bank building.

At the January 14, 1908, annual meeting of stockholders and officers, plans for interior remodeling of their

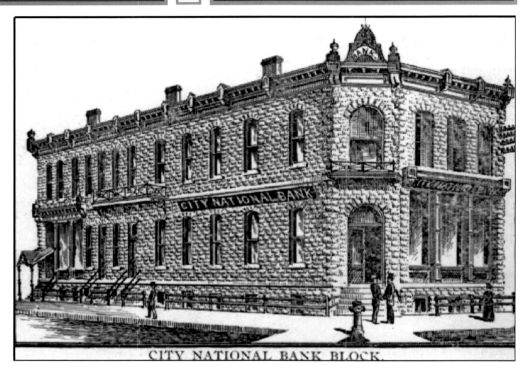

Drawing of the first City National Bank building at the corner of East State Street and South Main Street, 1892. Photograph Archive, digital file "City National Bank," Lee P. Loomis Archives, Mason City Public Library, Mason City, Iowa. (MCPL)

---

[2] *Mason City and Cerro Gordo County Directory* (Dubuque: Telegraph Herald Printing, 1908) 66.

[3] "A Brief History of the City National Bank of Mason City, Iowa," *Western Architect* 27:12, December 1911. In 2005 currency, the 1873 capital would have equaled approximately $789,000 increasing to $1,895,000 in 1883. The calculation is based on the Gross Domestic Product deflator which measures the average price of goods and services produced in the economy. Lawrence Officer and Samuel Williamson, "Relative Value in U.S. Dollars," 2007, 19 June 2007 <http://measuringworth.com>.

[4] "Mason City, Iowa: An Architectural Heritage," *Inventory of Historic and Architecturally Significant Buildings*, 1971. Reproduced in *Prairie School, Vol. I,,* Lee P. Loomis Archives, Mason City Public Library, Mason City, Iowa (Loomis Archives, MCPL)

[5] Ibid.

original bank building were proposed. An appointed committee explored the possibility for a new bank building to be located on the southwest corner of State and Main Streets. Bank officers and directors James S. Wheeler, J.E. Blythe, A.W. Dawson, State Senator A.H. Gale, J.F. Shaible, George W. Hill, J.E.E. Markley, J.E. Moore, and Mary Emsley Adams approved the purchase of lots across the street from their first bank. They proposed building a new, more fashionable bank on the property.[6]

Their choice to erect a new building may have been influenced by a competitor. In 1908, Charles McNider, soon to be the majority owner of the first cement plant, disclosed his intention to construct a new bank on the site of his original First National Bank on the northeast corner of the same State and Main intersection. The

bank with McNider as president was becoming the largest in Iowa at the time.[7]

The new City National Bank's prime site was the corner of the busiest street in all of Mason City. The lot first served as the lawn of George Brentner's residence in the 1860s. In the late 1860s, the lot hosted the city's first hotel and the first billiard table in the community. In 1870, William Weir purchased the 22-foot lot for $2,000, but conveyed it to his friend C.H. Day in 1874 to avoid litigation. Day refused to return it, holding ownership until 1903. Disputes with the Weir family surfaced in local courts, but Day retained the property. In 1877, he also purchased the 22-foot lot immediately south from George Virmilya.[8]

Over the years from 1871 to 1909, the lots served many businesses, including the West and Gregory Lumber firm, a saloon-pool room, barber shop, the Trafford Music Co. office, Haase Jewelry store, a harness shop, and a shoemaker shop. In 1894, J.C. Galico, manager of a successful restaurant on the corner, painted the exterior white with yellow spots.[9] Thus the name the "Yellow Spot."

"Yellow Spot" building at the corner of State and Main, 1909. Even though the spots were gone, the name stayed with the building until it was demolished. Photograph Archive, digital file "Park Inn Hotel," Loomis Archives, MCPL.

[6] "Plan for New Bank," unidentified newspaper article from 26 September 1908, reproduced in *Prairie School, Vol. I,* Loomis Archives, MCPL; "The Annual Meeting," *Mason City Globe Gazette* 14 January 2008.

[7] Dr. Robert McCoy, "Rock Crest/Rock Glen Prairie Planning in Iowa," *The Prairie School Review,* 5:3, 1968, 9. In the 1910 *History of Cerro Gordo County* by J.H. Wheeler (Chicago: Lewis Publishing), the name is consistently spelled "*McNider.*" That spelling was used by the family until General Hanford MacNider (1889-1966) changed it to more accurately reflect family history.

[8] "First Things in Mason City," *Mason City Times-Herald* 5 April 1909; "Old City National Bank Property, 'Lost' for 52 Years, Returns to Family," *Mason City Globe Gazette and Daily Times* 5 June 1926; "Mason City is Happy," *Mason City Times-Herald* 25 May 1906. [Sources conflict on whether Weir purchased it in 1870 or 1872.]

[9] "Old City National Bank Property, 'Lost' for 52 Years, Returns to Family"; "Why call it Yellow Spot?" *Mason City Times-Herald* 3 April 1909; "The Man Who Named The 'Yellow Spot,'" unidentified newspaper article 6 March 1909, *Prairie School Vol. 1,* Loomis Archives, MCPL.

In September of 1908, a business corporation of stockholders formed specifically to oversee the future of the City National Bank. The decision to move forward and construct a new bank rather than remodeling the old one came by the end of 1908. The capital stock of the City National Bank Building Company, fixed at $50,000, was scheduled to run for twenty years. J.S. Wheeler, bank president at the time, sold the property to the company.[10] Preliminary plans for the building encompassed the whole of the 44 x 82 foot lot. Bank's directors Markley and Blythe purchased the lot to the west on State Street. The two, both influential Mason City lawyers, secured an architect for the project.[11]

In January of 1909, the bank corporation settled on the proposed building plans and specifications. *The Mason City Times* reported that the new bank would begin construction in April of that year. The corner of State and Main was cleared by April 1, 1909. The Yellow Spot building would not be missed by the city. According to a 1907 article in the *Mason City Times-Herald*, the Yellow Spot "has just about as much right to exist as those which were condemned by our city council last winter."[12] and "The corner could be little else than a breeding place of disease from the conditions unearthed there by the demolishing of the old buildings."[13] The improvements to the block were a step forward for the city, estimated to aggregate more than $190,000 for the business center.[14]

The final architectural plans for the structure arrived on March 31, 1909,[15] just in time for the final clearing of the lot by April 1. One reporter wrote, "It is now possible to realize how great the extent of these two properties is and how large the new buildings to be erected there will be."[16] The architect was nationally-acclaimed Frank Lloyd Wright, a respected modernist whose other works were well- known, particularly in Chicago.

The new building plan, expanded to include law offices and a hotel to the west of the bank on the property owned by Markley and Blythe, boasted the utmost in modern architecture and convenience. A. H. Gale, president of the bank, indicated that the building would be only three stories high and built "according to the latest in design and architecture for buildings of that kind."[17] The choice of a building of three-story height for the City National Bank contrasted with McNider's First National Bank, which would stand eight stories tall. Instead of competing in height, the directors chose to focus on modern style and form. "It is the plan of the corporation to build a strictly bank building and not a skyscraper."[18] The focus on a small, down-to-earth bank building likely appealed to many.

City National Bank, 1909, before the new building was erected across the street. Photograph Archive, digital file "CNB," Loomis Archives, MCPL.

[10] "City Bank Building Co. Incorporated," *Mason City Times-Herald* 22 October 1908.

[11] "Plan for a New Bank."

[12] "Mason City is Happy."

[13] "Unsanitary Spot Exposed," *Mason City Globe Gazette* 31 April 1909.

[14] "The Old Yellow Spot Corner Will Soon Change," *Mason City Times-Herald* 6 March 1909.

[15] "Bank Plans Here," *Mason City Globe Gazette* 31 March 1909.

[16] "Yellow Spot Corner Clear by April 1st," *Mason City Times-Herald* 22 March 1909.

[17] "City National will build April first," *Mason City Times-Herald* 22 January 1909.

[18] "Plan for a New Bank."

Blythe, Markley, Rule and Smith

The law firm of Blythe, Markley, Rule and Smith played a critical role in the development of the City National Bank and Park Inn Hotel. Conceived in 1869, the law firm grew from a prominent and respected firm of the time, Goodykoontz and Wilbur. In the late 1870s Goodykoontz and Wilber's partnership dissolved. Then in 1878 Blythe took the position as partner to Goodykoontz.[19]

James E. Blythe was born in Cranberry, New Jersey, in 1856. After graduation from Hanover College in Indiana, Blythe moved to Mason City to read law in the Goodykoontz and Wilbur office. In 1881, Blythe married Grace Smith and raised two girls, Maude and Jean.[20] Blythe, known for his skill as an orator, was regarded as a "strong" candidate for Congress due to his "extensive political acquaintance and experience in public affairs."[21] In the 1920s, Blythe's fellow Republicans called upon him to run for governor. Although he never accepted the appeal, Blythe worked as the successful campaign manager for two governors. The *Des Moines Capital* wrote, "He is by all odds the best political manager Iowa has developed in twenty-five years."[22] Blythe was also active in developing Mason City, including the Cecil Theatre as well as the City National Bank and Park

James Blythe, 1896. Photograph Archive, digital file "Misc," Loomis Archives,

Inn Hotel with partner James Markley.[23] Blythe died at the age of eighty-two in September 1938.[24]

Later in 1878, Edward Wheeler joined Goodykoontz and Blythe's practice. According to a history of the firm, the "lawyers were well trained and of pronounced ability in their exacting profession." The respected firm continued to do well in the 1880s. Wheeler left the firm in 1881, but his place was quickly filled by Markley.[25]

James Edward Earle Markley was born in Knox County, Ohio, in 1857, then moved with his family to Cedar Falls, Iowa, at the age of nine. At seventeen, Markley attended Cornell College where he received his Bachelor's degree. He attended law school at the University of Iowa, graduating in 1878 and beginning practice in 1879 in Marshalltown, Iowa. In September of 1881, Blythe recruited Markley to Mason City. Not long after, he became a partner in the firm, creating Goodykoontz, Blythe and Markley.[26]

---

[19] *History of Franklin and Cerro Gordo County* (Springfield, IL: Union Publishing Co., 1883) 633.

[20] *Who's Who in Mason City Iowa*, local publication, 1929, Loomis Archives, MCPL.

[21] "Mr. Blythe's Public Career," *Mason City Globe Gazette* 17 May 1920.

[22] Ibid.

[23] "Meet James Blythe," *Mason City Globe Gazette* 19 November 1927.

[24] Obituary Index, "B," Loomis Archives, MCPL.

[25] J.H. Wheeler, *History of Cerro Gordo County, Iowa. Vol. II* (Chicago: Lewis Publishing Co. 1910) 441.

[26] Ibid, 590.

A staunch supporter of the Democratic Party, Markley was once suggested for Congress as he "possess[ed] the qualifications in eminent degree, and who, if he would consent to be a candidate, would unite and crystallize the Democratic strength and sentiment of the district as no other man could at this time."[27] He was a well-respected lawyer known for his skill at public speaking. On May 1, 1888, he married Miss Lilly Emsley, daughter of the founder of the City National Bank. He had two daughters, Marion and Doris. Blythe and Markley both contrib-

J.E.E. Markley. Vertical file, "Markley Family Scrapbook," Loomis Archives, MCPL.

uted to Mason City, developing and owning many properties together. Markley died on October 19, 1939, at the age of eighty-two.[28]

Under the supervision of Blythe and Markley, the firm grew to great acclaim and respect in the city. Other partnerships formed over the years; however, Blythe and Markley remained the only two principal figures throughout its history. The firm of Blythe, Markley, and Smith was created when Clifford Smith joined the two prominent Mason City lawyers in 1895. Only five years later Smith would retire. A. S. Rinard, a former county attorney, practiced briefly with Blythe and Markley before taking a position as a district judge. Thus, the partnership was limited to only Blythe and Markley until 1903 when Arthur L. Rule was admitted. In 1905 Clarence H. Smith was hired, finally forming the well-known firm of Blythe, Markley, Rule and Smith.[29]

Rule, a Mason City native, received his education at Northwestern University in Evanston, Illinois. When the Spanish-American war broke out, he volunteered as quarter master for the staff of General Lincoln and achieved the rank of colonel. In 1889, Rule entered law school at the University of Iowa; after graduation he worked in Cedar Rapids. Rule moved to Mason City with his wife Edith and daughter Edith in 1902, joining Blythe and Markley shortly thereafter.[30] Clarence Smith, also a native of Mason City, joined the firm in 1905 as a stenographer and clerk. He passed the law board examination in 1905 and was formally admitted to the firm as a partner. Smith, an active member of Mason City society, owned stock in the Commercial Savings Bank and Mason City Building and Loan Association.[31]

Blythe, Markley, Rule and Smith continued as one of the most respected and sought-after firms in Mason City, holding a "place of marked priority" for their "highest professional standard through the fine character and distinctive ability of its interested principals."[32] By the early 1900s, the growing law business, one "of the largest in the state,"[33] made it necessary for Blythe and Markley, the senior partners of their firm, to expand to more comfortable and lavish quarters. Blythe and Markley, also stockholders in the City National Bank, wanted to commission a work that would include a new bank to compete with McNider's First National Bank, improved law offices for the firm, a hotel, rental offices and mercantile space. In 1908, they set about selecting an architect to design a modern, multipurpose structure to match the firm's high standards.

[27] "Markley Family Scrapbook (green cover), Loomis Archives, MCPL.
[28] Obituary index, "L-M," Loomis Archives, MCPL.
[29] Wheeler, 590.
[30] Ibid, 624-25.
[31] Ibid, 603-604
[32] Ibid, 441.
[33] Ibid.

From left to right: Blythe, Markley, and Smith c. 1920. Arthur Rule c.1920. Photograph Archive, digital file "Prairie School People," Loomis Archives, MCPL.

The Architect

Frank Lloyd Wright entered the picture through J.E.E. Markley whose daughters Marion and Doris attended the Hillside Home School in Spring Green, Wisconsin. Jane and Ellen Lloyd Jones, the aunts of Frank Lloyd Wright, operated the school. In 1902 when Markley's eldest daughter entered Hillside, Wright had just completed his aunts' second building, a magnificent stone structure in the Prairie School style. Markley and Wright became friends. In 1908 Wright received the bank and hotel commission.[34]

Blythe and Markley's choice of Wright as their architect for a bank, office and hotel building may well have been influenced by his growing reputation, but they could hardly know the world-wide acclaim he would one day achieve. After a brief apprenticeship in 1877 with Lyman Silsbee, who designed in the American Shingle Style, Wright joined the architectural firm of Adler and Sullivan, quickly becoming Louis Sullivan's head draftsman. There he did most of the firm's residential designs and began to develop his style that emphasized horizontal strength, letting function determine form, inspired by Sullivan to develop an American architectural style free of European influence. Dismissed in 1893 for moonlighting, Wright added his Oak Park studio as an extension of his home. With the help of his staff, including Marion Mahony, Walter Burley Griffin, Barry Byrne and William Drummond, the studio produced over 120 early Prairie period designs.[35]

"Markley Family Photograph," Doris and Marion are on the right side. Photograph Archive, digital file "Markley," Loomis Archives, MCPL.

---

[34] Dr. Robert McCoy, interview 19 June 3 1965 with Ralph Lloyd Jones, cousin of Frank Lloyd Wright who attended Hillside School with Marion Markley.

[35] Wright's work with Silsbee and Sullivan, his style, and his associates are detailed in Brendon Gill's *Many Masks: A Life of Frank Lloyd Wright* (New York: Ballantine Books, 1987) 56-86, 185-190.

Wright's work with Louis Sullivan and his love of organic expression made him the forerunner of a new modern American style. The early works of Wright, located primarily in the Chicago area, date from the early 1890s to 1909. In numbers, this Prairie Style was used mostly for residential commissions; however, three of his greatest non-residential achievements, the Larkin Building, Unity Temple and the City National Bank and Hotel, were among this period's major works. His City National Bank and Hotel design stands on the cusp between his Prairie School period and the period that would produce Midway Gardens and the Imperial Hotel.[36]

The Prairie School style was based on the development of a strong relationship to the horizontal nature of the prairie, gaining its horizontal strength from low-pitched, broadly-projecting hip roofs with broad low chimneys, strong horizontal moldings and bands of windows. Strong baseboard skirts or water tables made the foundations invisible, so the structure appeared "of the earth." Interiors had openly flowing spaces with a central focal point such as a hearth, using natural materials like wood, stone, brick and terra cotta. To Wright, the Prairie School style was "founded very directly on the climate, land forms, and life-style of the region." The use of abstracted nature in his window designs was one way Wright could make nature and the built environment unite. He wrote, "A knowledge of cause and effect in line, color and form, as found in organic nature, furnishes guide lines within which an artist may sift materials, test motives and direct aims. . ."[37]

Challenged as he was by Sullivan to develop that American architectural style without European reference, Wright also gradually gained inspiration from Japanese art and architecture and to a lesser degree, Meso-American elements of style. Attention to detail, handcrafted design and use of natural materials came partly through the examples in William Morris's Arts and Crafts movement of the 1880s. Wright was also influenced by the half-scale exhibit of the Japanese Government pavilion Ho-o-den at the Chicago World's Fair of 1893. After visiting Japan with Ward Willits in 1905, the architect wrote: "Japanese art, I found, really did have organic character, was nearer to earth and a more indigenous product of native conditions of life and work and therefore more nearly modern as I saw it, than European civilizations alive or dead."[38]

Frank Lloyd Wright. Photograph Archive, digital file "Famous People," Loomis Archives, MCPL.

[36] Dr. Robert McCoy, interview July 2007, Mason City, Iowa.

[37] Frank Lloyd Wright, *Buildings Plans and Designs* (New York: Horizon Press Publishers, 1957).

[38] Richard Guy Wilson and Sidney Robinson, *The Prairie School in Iowa* (Ames: Iowa State University Press, 1977) 6-7; In 1901, Wright designed a home in Highland Park, Illinois, for Ward Willits. It was Wright's first true Prairie Style house. Willits, president of the brass and bronze factory Adams and Westlake Company, and his wife accompanied the Wrights on their first trip to Japan in 1905. "Wright's Illinois Work," 13 August 2009, <http://www.dgunning.org/architecture/Illinois/willits.htm?>.

The Design

The City National Bank and Hotel building was the third major non-domestic commission of Wright's Prairie period. The City National Bank was his second bank design,[39] and the Park Inn Hotel is the last remaining hotel of the six he designed. The larg-est and most famous was the Imperial Hotel in Tokyo, built across the moat from the Imperial Palace at the Emperor Taisho's request. In its day, it was one of the most famous hotels in the world.[40]

The three main functions of the structure are expressed in this rendering from the Wasmuth portfolio. The bank portion is to the far left and the hotel to the far right. The recessed portion or waist between the two ends contained the law office of Blythe and Markley, entered by the ground-floor entrance in the building's center. *Ausgefuhrte Bauten und Entwurfe von Frank Lloyd Wright,* **Berlin, Ernst Wasmuth, 1911.**

---

[39] The Larkin Building (1903) in Buffalo, New York, and Unity Church (1904) were Wright's prior major non-residential achievements. The First National Bank (1905) Dwight, Illinois, was his first bank building. *WRIGHT ON THE WEB*, 9 July 2009 <http://www.delmars.com/wright/flw3.htm.>.

[40] The other five hotels: the Horseshoe Inn 1908; Como Orchard Clubhouse (Inn) 1908; the Bitter Root Inn 1908; Lake Geneva Hotel 1911; the Imperial Hotel 1915-1923 and Annex 1919. William Allin Storrer, *The Frank Lloyd Wright Companion* (Chicago and London: Oxford University Press), 1993, 144-147, 172, 196-198. However, Storrer's *FL^LW Update,* 10 July 2009 <http://www.franklloydwrightinfo.comdamietta.html> concludes that the Horseshoe Inn design intended for Estes Park, Colorado, was never actually built.

City National Bank building, 1910 postcard. Photograph Archive, digital file "CNB," Loomis Archives, MCPL.

Wright's commission was a challenging one: a building to fulfill the functions of bank, hotel, law offices for the developers, rental office and retail shop space in one coherent design. Wright's insistence that form must follow function can be seen in the way the architect defined the spaces. As photos and drawings show, the bank structure, facing Main Street (now Federal Avenue) on the east and the hotel, adjacent to the bank but facing north, are clearly defined as two separate, differently functioning spaces joined by a narrower waist and unified by varying design elements.

15

The City National Bank[41] had a two-story banking room with the top floor dedicated to rental offices. Wright described its relationship of form to function: "As a banking institution should be an expression of integrity in its nature, the materials of which it was built were honestly used with no veneers or facings or fake columns or fake architecture that has to be made just for effect."[42]

High buff-brick walls with an elevated, recessed entry as a focal point characterized the main facade. A horizontal stone belt course unified the sills of the high banking windows. The appearance of a second floor misled the observer, as clerestory windows brought natural light into the banking rooms and provided for a sixteen-foot high ceiling. The second floor (what would have appeared to be the third floor) housed rental office space. The upper-floor east facade had five large, single-pane windows separated by vertical brick columns. The north facade had nine windows. Ornamental colored terra cotta tiles adorned the upper shafts of the brick columns, adding color to the otherwise plain exterior. A wide eave, typical of the Prairie style, capped the structure.[43]

When they entered the bank, customers saw

This drawing of the City National Bank's exterior appeared in *Ausgefuhrte Bauten und Entwurfe von Frank Lloyd Wright,* **Berlin: Ernst Wasmuth, 1911.**

[41] Over the years some sections remained as first designed while others were altered dramatically. The 2009-2011 rehabilitation returns some of these to the original intent. In this section, the original building is presented in past tense for consistency.

[42] "A Brief History of the City National Bank of Mason City, Iowa." "City National Bank Moves to Its New Home," *Mason City Times,* November 1910.

[43] Ibid.

Interior of the City National Bank showing teller cages and clerestory windows. Photo taken for *Western Architect*, Dec. 1911. Photograph Archive, digital file "CNB," Loomis Archives, MCPL.

three tellers' windows placed in the center of the large banking room. A fire-proof, freestanding brick vault rose behind the teller island. The stone slab vault top sat at the same height as the clerestory windows. Four bronze statues of Mercury by Richard Bock, a long-time friend and colleague of Wright, rose from the teller island. Prairie school urns placed on freestanding piers at the corner of the banking area as decorative elements enhanced the rectangular design. Other ornamental elements included the decorative clerestory window grilles and the art-glass skylights over the officers' rooms. The president, cashier and directors had rooms in the one-story extension to the south of the banking floor. The only natural light that entered the office spaces came from the skylights and art-glass windows to the north between the banking room and offices.[44]

[44] Ibid.

[45] Richard Bock was born in Germany and immigrated to the United States at age four. His first job was working on plaster, stone, and woodcarvings for the Vanderbilt Mansion. To increase his skills he took a grand tour of Europe, studying under master sculptors. Among his noted works were the Grecian figures on Solon Beman's Mining and Metallurgy Building, 1893, Chicago World's Fair. Bock met Wright while working in Sullivan's office; their first collaboration was on the Heller House in 1897. Afterwards, Bock was Wright's favorite sculptor. "Versatile and inventive, his styles embraced classical, abstract, and Art Nouveau." Jeanette Fields, "Bock to the Future," *Wright Plus Journal*, n.d. *Prairie School, Vol. II*, Loomis Archives, MCPL. Wright wrote about "The Spirit of Mercury," as he called the light fixtures: "Mercury . . . fostered abundance and prosperity, and consequently was adopted as the patron of commerce and finance. . . The figure (rises) straight like a plant out of the ground, assuming shape as it develops and crystallizes . . . emphasized by the chrystal forms clinging to the figure much in the nature of a chrysalis. " Frank Lloyd Wright, "City National Bank of Mason City, Iowa," *The Western Architect 27:105 (*December, 1911).

"Spirit of Mercury" bank light fixtures contained statues of Mercury designed by Richard Bock.[45] Photos taken for *Western Architect,* Dec. 1911. Photograph Archive, digital file "CNB," Loomis Archives, MCPL.

Interior of the bank directors' room with art-glass ceiling and wall as well as Wright-designed furniture. Photo taken for *Western Architect*, Dec. 1911. Photograph Archive, digital file "CNB," Loomis Archives, MCPL.

The architect discussed the purpose of his design in the following excerpt from *The Western Architect*: [46]

> *The building for the City National Bank of Mason City was designed with the idea that a bank building is itself a strong box on a large scale; a well aired and lighted fire proof vault. The problem was complicated by commercial consideration of offices overhead, for rent . . . The bank room itself was moved aside from the party line to insure light and air on all sides; the round space thus left was utilized for office quarters. By this means a continuous border of windows was carried around the high banking room at the ceiling, affording light with perfect distribution as well as good ventilation. These windows form a frieze of light within the bank room; they combine with the office windows in the frieze which the whole superstructure becomes on the outside; the walls of the bank, sixteen feet above the sidewalk, are a solid mass unbroken by openings save the entrance. The entrance and upper windows are guarded by heavy bronze castings so that the bank, itself, is a strong box splendidly lighted and ventilated.*

Nationally, Wright designed only one other bank building. Built in 1905 in Dwight, Illinois, as a single-purpose edifice,[47] it differed strikingly from the City National Bank and Hotel, designed and built as one harmonious structure with its two sections somewhat differentiated. Form followed function. The hotel was the more dynamic and inviting space with two entrances at grade level. Its multiple roof levels on the recessed central section progressed in height

---

[46]"Frank Lloyd Wright, "City National Bank of Mason City, Iowa."

[47]"First National Bank of Dwight," brochure, n.d. Available at the Wright on the Park Inc. office, Mason City, Iowa. Wright also designed "A Village Bank," published in the *Brickbuilder* (Wilson, p. 10) but apparently it was never built.

from front to back, contained by the three-story lateral wings. Symmetric stairwell towers on both sides added to the effect. A central light court brightened the art-glass dining room ceiling.

The banking area, four steps above grade facing Main Street, was divorced from the hotel and restaurant by the deep waist or recess in the park-facing facade. This elevated and recessed area provided entry to first-floor retail shops and to the law firm of Blythe, Markley, Rule and Smith on the second floor and to the rental offices above the bank building. Nevertheless, the bank and hotel united through their heavy projecting roof lines, hori-

Cook-Montgomery Co. postcard of the Park Inn Hotel, c. 1911. Photograph Archive, digital file "Park Inn Hotel," Loomis Archives, MCPL.

zontal stone moldings and the choice of building materials. Buff-colored brick with deeply-raked horizontal mortar joints further emphasized the horizontal strength of design. Polychrome and terra cotta tiles added color to the north facade and repeated the tile ornament of the bank. Wright wrote, "The building is situated on a prominent corner, opposite the central park of the city, a city in which the buildings were rather cheerless in character, so quiet-colored ceramic inlays were used to brighten the exterior."[48]

The building was indeed opposite Central Park, a well-maintained open space. The placement of the long axis of the hotel on State Street gave it a distinctly different flavor from the bank, which faced the bustling Main Street. The entrances to the hotel, located at sidewalk level, faced the park. Symbolically, the hotel became a place of tranquility compared to the noisy commercial center.

---

[48] Wright, "City National Bank of Mason City, Iowa."

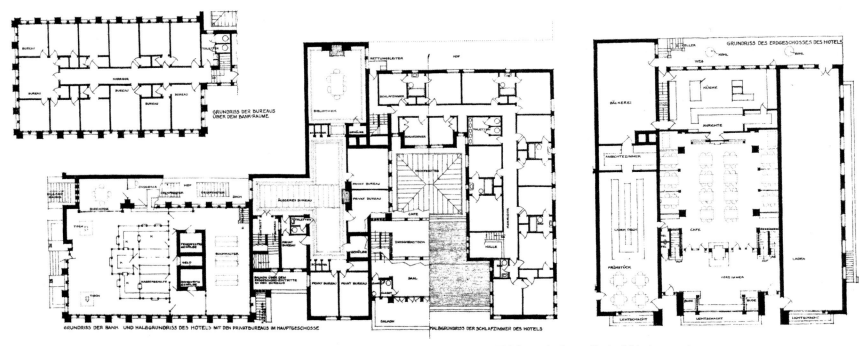

Floor plans from the Wasmuth Portfolio. The original floor plans by Wright are in Appendix A of this document.

The floor-use designations in the working drawings and 1911 *Western Architect* magazine[49] agree for the most part. In the initial hotel space allocation, the first-floor west bay was to be a newspaper office with the press room in the basement. Guest rooms were above on the second and third floors. While drawings vary on the purpose of the first-floor east bay, the original shows a breakfast room, lunch room and bakery there. Law offices occupied the second floor of the east wing with their sidewalk entrance below in the central waist. Wright labeled the space on the first floor beneath the skylight "Café," with the hotel lobby in front, a kitchen in the rear and a mezzanine balcony looking north into the lobby and south into the café. Above the lobby a "Ladies Parlor" opened on to a balcony cantilevered over the sidewalk facing Central Park. Two ornamental urns capped the balcony corners.

In all, the hotel held forty-three available sleeping rooms: 14 guest rooms on the second floor, 22 on the third and 7 house staff rooms. Typically, room size was 100 square feet. Most often two rooms shared a bath located between them. However, other rooms shared bathrooms located off the hallway.

---

[49]*Ausgefuhrte Bauten und Entwurfe von Frank Lloyd Wright (*Berlin: Ernst Wasmuth, 1911.) The description on this and the following page is distilled from these various floor-plan sources, with interpretations by Dr. Robert McCoy, AIA (hon), past member, Frank Lloyd Wright Building Conservancy. The newspaper office and press room never materialized. It was likely intended for the *Times-Herald,* in bankruptcy by 1897 when its property sold. It managed to continue publishing under varied ownerships until Emory English of Des Moines finally became editor and part owner. But instead of locating in the hotel building, in 1910 Emory erected a new *Times* Building south of the hotel. In 1918, the *Times* was purchased and merged with the *Globe Gazette*. Centennial Edition, *Mason City Globe Gazette* 1 June 1953, p. 16, 21.

When a patron entered the lobby, the registration desk sat in the center with stairs on either side set off by open screens of vertical square spindles. Two sets of art-glass accordion doors opened into the dining area lit by the art-glass ceiling designed by Wright. Behind the café was the logical place for the kitchen. The mezzanine balcony, located directly above the registration desk, provided a walkway between stairwells, a chance for guests to survey the dining room and lobby from above and a place for musicians to entertain diners.

Above the lobby, the second-floor stairwell opened to the ladies' parlor. A loggia of five art-glass double French doors to the north of the parlor provided access to the balcony overlooking Central Park. To the south of the parlor, two sample rooms were used by traveling salesmen to demonstrate house wares, fabrics and other items for the ladies to order.

The eastern portion of the second floor held the law offices of Blythe, Markley, Rule and Smith. Each member of the firm had his own office. Two offices faced Central Park and measured approximately 14 feet by 11 feet. A large office overlooked the light court. This office most likely belonged to Mr. Blythe, senior partner of the firm. The spacious law library directly adjacent to Blythe's office to the south also overlooked the central light court and had a handsome fireplace made from bricks fired at a brick factory in Fertile, Iowa. A large main office room for clients measured 30 by 30 feet with the vault opening on its west side. Mahogany furnishings and wood trim created a rich, inviting space.[50]

The gentlemen's lounge was located in the basement level. The area provided male guests with a place to discuss current events, business and other matters of the day. Natural light came through tall windows in light wells below the front sidewalk. A curb, brass railing and projecting brick piers protected the light wells. Undefined space to the east and west offered storage for the hotel. The boiler room, coal room and laundry rooms occupied the rear of the basement.

Bank vault in City National Bank. *Western Architect, 1911.* **Photograph Archive, digital file "CNB," Loomis Archives. MCPL.**

---

[50] "Old Legal Firm in New Offices," *Mason City Times* 29 August 1910.

The Significance

Frank Lloyd Wright's City National Bank and Hotel[51] ranks as significant locally, nationally and internationally. Locally, his designs sparked a Prairie School movement in the city. Several blocks east of the hotel and bank, the Rock Crest/Rock Glen neighborhood emerged as a premiere example of Prairie School style. The first house was built for Dr. G.C. Stockman. Wright saw this home through to completion in 1908, but he was not present for the bank and hotel's completion because he ran off to Europe with Mamah Cheney. Already supervising on-site, Wright's Chicago associate William Drummond oversaw the work.[52]

The full Prairie School neighborhood, with Willow Creek running between its high and low banks, was initiated by Blythe, Markley, Joshua Melson and W.J. Holahan under the inspiration of Walter Burley Griffin, another Wright associate. Wright had already designed a house for Melson, who did not approve a final plan before the scandalous elopement. Melson then asked Griffin for a house designed to appear as an upward extension of the sheer cliff on the south side of the creek. The plan to build Prairie Style homes on the cliff and glen side of Willow Creek escalated. If not for his sudden department, Wright might well have been an integral part of that development. William Storrer wrote, "Had Wright been present . . . Blythe might have become the kind of client that so often failed to materialize for the architect, one with many commissions at his hand."[53] In 1999, Jon Lipman, representing the Frank Lloyd Wright Building Conservancy, told the city council, "(This) is the major focus of Prairie architecture outside of Chicago . . . the largest collection of Prairie School houses unified by a common natural setting in the world."[54]

Top: **The home Wright designed for Dr. G.C. Stockman.** *Above:* **Joshua Melson home designed in the Prairie School style by Walter Burley Griffin. Photos by Dr. Robert McCoy.**

[51] The building was always referred to as the "City National Bank and Hotel" by Frank Lloyd Wright. It was not until the hotel opened in September 1910 that it was called the Park Inn Hotel.

[52] Wilson, p. 10.

[53] The Prairie School style homes in Mason City are described in detail by Dr. Robert McCoy, "Rock Creek/Rock Glenn: Prairie School Planning in Iowa," 5-39; William Storrer, p. 159.

[54] Jon Lipman, City Council meeting speech, 3 March 1999, Mason City, Iowa.

The Park Inn Hotel is the only Wright-designed hotel remaining in the world.[55] It is a pivotal building between his Prairie School period and the decade to follow in which he designed Midway Gardens and the Imperial Hotel. With the Prairie period's Larkin Building and Unity Temple, it shares the combination of two building segments of dissimilar function in which each segment is symmetric within itself yet the two contribute to the symmetry of the building as a whole. Like the City National Bank and Hotel, the other two are joined by a narrower waist containing the principal entrance - front and back in free-standing Larkin and Unity Temple and only on the north side in the City National Bank and Hotel because the bank's back is against the building to the rear. The Park Inn Hotel shares similar massing with Midway Gardens and the Imperial Hotel. The central section of the hotel rises stepwise from front to back while being contained by two flanking lateral wings as high as the highest point at the rear. It is assisted in this containment by the stair towers along the medial edges of the lateral wings. This is similar to Midway Gardens' massing when looking south from the orchestra stage. The Imperial Hotel and Park Inn Hotel are similar in their massing when seen from the front.[56]

Top : **Midway Gardens ballroom seen from the performing stage. June 2007 <http://wwwplanetclair.org/flw/img.html >.** *Above:* **Imperial Hotel luggage tag. Courtesy of Bergland and Cram Architects, Mason City, Iowa.**

---

[55] Wright participated in the design of the hotel now called the Arizona Biltmore which opened in Phoenix in 1929. However, the main architect was Albert Chase McArther, who had worked as a draftsman for Wright. "Arizona Biltmore Resort and Spa, 10 July 2009 <http://www.arizonaguide.com/DisplayListing.aspx?id=5296>.

[56] Dr. Robert McCoy, interpretation of photographs, June 2007 interview, Mason City, Iowa. Midway Gardens opened in Chicago in 1913. "Frank Lloyd Wright: Midway Gardens, 11 July 2009 <http://www.planetclaire.org/flw/Mg.html>. The Imperial Hotel in Tokyo was commissioned in 1916 and demolished in 1968. "Imperial Hotel: 1912-1923," 11 July 2009 <http://ww,obs,irg.fkw.byukdubgs.Unoeruak?Imperial.html>.

Internationally, the hotel design sparked considerable interest in Europe. In 1910, Ernst Wasmuth, Berlin, Germany, published photographs of Wright's built works in *Ausgefuhrte Bauten;* and in 1911, Wasmuth published a large two-volume folio edition of Wright's revised presentation drawings of his buildings through 1909 as *Ausgefuhrte Bauten und Entwurfe von Frank Lloyd Wright.* Working on the latter for publication became Wright's primary project in Europe in 1909 and 1910. Coming after its publication, Walter Gropius and Adolph Meyer's pavilion built for the 1914 *Deutscher Werkbund* exhibition in Cologne reflects Wright's international influence.[57] "Frank Lloyd Wright's career paralleled and influenced the work of the European modernists (led by Le Corbusier in France, Gropius and Mies van der Rohe in Germany), particularly via the Wasmuth Portfolio, but he refused to be categorized with them. (He) was a major influence on Gropius and Van der Rohe (both directors of the Bauhaus School) as well as on the whole of organic architecture."[58]

Left: **1914 Model Factory by Gropius, located in Cologne, Germany.** *Below:* **The Park Inn Hotel, c. 1911. In his book *Modern Architecture: The Architecture of Democracy* (New York: George Braziller, Inc., 1961) pp. 25-26, 60, Vincent Scully pointed out the similarity of the designs as illustration of Wright's influence on the international scene. Reprinted with permission George Braziller, Inc.**

[57] Walter Gropius and Adolf Meyer's "Model Factory" was designed for the Deutscher Werkbund Cologne Exhibition of 1914 as one of the buildings exemplifying artistic industrialization. Influenced by Wright's work, Gropius went on to found the Bauhaus School of Architecture in Germany. He fled Nazi Germany in 1928. Sue Osgood, "Bauhaus defined," *Helium,* 10 July 2009 <http:www.helium.com/items/1248880-bauhaus-defined>.

[58] "Modern Architecture," *Absolute Astronomy.com: Exploring the universe of knowledge,* 10 July 2009 <http://www.absoluteastronomy.com/topics/Modern_artchitecture>. Numerous sources recount the day the portfolio reached the Berlin office of Peter Behrens, where reportedly all 20 plus of his apprentices (including Walter Gropius, Charles-Eduard Jenneret and Mies van der Rohe) closed the office to pour over the volume. Van der Rohe said, "Wright's work presented an architectural world of unexpected force, clarity of language and disconcerting richness of form." "Frank Lloyd Wright's Wasmuth Portfolio," Exhibition Archive, *ArchiTech* 13 September 2009 <http://www.architechgallery.com>.

Completion of the City National Bank and Park Inn Hotel

The approval of Wright's design by Blythe, Markley and the City National Bank corporation occurred in January of 1909 with the clearing of previous buildings completed on the lot April 1 of that year. Architect William Drummond saw the City National Bank and Park Inn Hotel through to completion. He was already working as the on-site supervisor of the project when Wright eloped to Europe with Mrs. Martha (Mamah) Borthwick Cheney, the wife of a former client.[59] Wright's abandonment of his wife, Catherine Clark Tobin Wright, and their six children made national headlines. In Mason City, the scandal prompted equally outraged newspaper stories.[60]

Drummond, a talented architect himself, had worked with Sullivan and later Wright.[61] Under his supervision, construction continued. The law firm moved into unfinished offices in August of 1910. On September 10, 1910, Blythe and Markley officially opened the hotel for business. In November of that year, the City National Bank formally moved into the new building.[62] In the end, the hotel was completed at a cost of $90,000 and the bank at a cost of $65,000.[63]

Regardless of the Wright scandal, the structure met with great acclaim from the press and public and prospered for twelve years. After the grand opening in 1910, however, the bank and hotel experienced drastically different fates.

Postcard of the completed City National Bank and Park Inn Hotel. Photograph archive, digital file "Park Inn," Loomis Archives, MCPL

[59] McCoy, "Rock Crest/Rock Glen Prairie Planning in Iowa," 12.

[60] Wilson, p. 12. The Nov. 9, 1910, Mason City newspaper's headline read "The Eloping Architect Known Here," and the story noted, "He was here frequently while attending to (his) work." Quoting the *Chicago Tribune*, the article noted that Wright considered his "not a tawdry elopement. . . but a spiritual hegira." Most of the rest of the world didn't see it quite that way. (unidentified newspaper, Loomis Archives, MCPL.)

[61] William Drummond worked in the office of Louis Sullivan for several months before joining the studio of Frank Lloyd Wright in 1899. He was the chief draftsman for several of Wright's commissions before obtaining his architect's license in 1901. He worked with Wright until a dispute over pay prompted his departure. "William Drummond," 11 July 2009 <http://www.prairiestyles.com/drummond.htm>. The Curtis Yelland house in the Rock Crest/Rock Glen neighborhood, east of the City National Bank in Mason City, was designed by Drummond while he was supervising the construction of the bank and hotel. McCoy, "Rock Crest/Rock Glen Prairie Planning in Iowa," 12.

[62] Wilson, p. 12.

[63] In 2005 currency, it would have required $5,940,000.00 to construct the City National Bank, and $8,225,581 to build the Park Inn Hotel. The calculation is based on the unskilled wage calculator which measures the relative cost of something by the amount of work it would take to produce today. Lawrence Officer and Samuel Williamson, "Relative Value in U.S. Dollars," 2007, 19 June 2007 <http://measuringworth.com>.

City National Bank 1910-2010

The opening of the City National Bank was welcomed with praise. The Mason City press described the interior space as having private viewing for vault boxes and offices for patrons. The mahog-any tellers' boxes and directors' offices "harmonized well with the design of the bank." An impressed reporter called the City National Bank, although modern in style, "a classic." The article concluded

The City National Bank *Western Architect*, Dec. 1911. Photograph Archive, digital file "CNB," Loomis Archives, MCPL.

that the bank would be a valuable asset to the community and a model for other architects' designs.[64] Wright wrote, "The City National Bank has established quite a precedent which if quietly and intelligently followed will make the city environment a pleasanter, happier thing in which to live."[65]

The City National Bank and its directors saw prosperous years after the opening of the bank. The success of the bank is difficult to measure; however, the small business seemed to hold its own initially against the First National Bank across the street. Newspapers recounted only minor mishaps; one in particular highlighted an unusual difficulty Frank Lloyd Wright's building experienced. In May of 1914, the *Mason City Times* reported that the office of director A. M. Rule flooded when dirty linens thrown out by a hotel maid clogged up the bank's "antique" roof drains while Rule's literature and papers were submerged in a flood of rain water.[66]

The continued success of the bank can be assessed in the remodeling of the banking rooms and offices in 1917. Estimated at $8,000, the 1917 remodeling provided each executive officer with a private office and a private room for customers as well as a new ladies' room. The bank expanded to the west into the space previously held by the Shepard Abstract company, nearly doubling the working area to the rear of the bank. Tellers' windows increased from three to seven, and the vault enlarged when bookkeepers moved to the new mezzanine floor over the vault. These expansions to major spaces indicate that the bank indeed profited from 1910-1917.[67]

Four years later, in 1921, the City National Bank and Commercial Savings Bank merged to form the City-Commercial Savings Bank. According to the *Mason City Globe Gazette*, the City National Bank proposed remodeling the floor in order to accommodate increased business. During the remodeling, business would be conducted at the Commercial Saving's Bank down the block. The remodeling plan also included an expansion of the bookkeeping department and two additional tellers cages.[68]

However, the proposed remodeling did not take place. In the 1920s the farming industry experienced a major economic downturn that led to the closing of numerous banks in Iowa. County banks found it difficult to renew bank notes to customers even prior to the 1920s farm crash. Typically, at this time banks loaned more money than they maintained, making the banking market unstable. In May of 1920, the government withdrew federal guarantees on wheat, causing the grain market to plummet; price supports for other crops quickly fell as well. Banks across Iowa slowly closed.

---

[64] "City National Bank Moves to its New Home," 9 November 1910, newspaper article reproduced in *Prairie School Vol. 1,* Loomis Archives, MCPL.

[65] "Frank Lloyd Wright Designed Homes Here," *Mason City Globe Gazette* April 1959. Quoting Frank Lloyd Wright.

[66] "Stock in National Bank Building Watered," *Mason City Times* 30 May 1914. The hotel also made *The Times-Herald* news 25 August 1913 with the headline "Canned Cook Steals Ham from Hotel." The fired chef stole a waiter's coat, in which he wrapped a stolen ham and took it to the Decker Restaurant to sell. He was later convicted of his crime.

[67] "City National Remodeled its Banking Rooms," *Mason City Globe Gazette* 31 December 1917.

[68] "2 Banks to merge coming Saturday," *Mason City Globe Gazette* 15 February 1921, 5.

City National Bank counter check. Photograph Archive, digital file "CNB," Loomis Archives, MCPL.

In 1920, 67 Iowa banks closed; the number increased to 505 in 1921; and in 1922, 366 banks shut their doors. In the remaining years of the 1920s, large numbers of banks failed each year.[69] The City-Commercial Savings Bank's location at 21-23 South Federal Avenue in the 1922-1925 Mason City Directory indicated the business never completed its remodeling or moved back into the City National Bank building. In 1926, the bank remained at the same 21-23 Federal Avenue location, but in receivership under L.A. Andrews, suggesting the bank declared bankruptcy between 1925 and 1926. McNider's First National remained the only bank in Mason City after the 1926 economic slump. The number of banks in Mason City had gone from five to one.[70]

In 1925, J.E.E Markley made arrangements to sell the City National Bank building. Argument over the purchase of the bank building erupted in 1926 when A.A. Adams, to whom the banking superintendent and receivership representative had agreed to sell it, backed out of the purchase. Adams claimed that the contract prepared by Markley was an option to buy the building, not an actual agreement to purchase. However, investigation revealed that Adams had taken out a $100,000 loan to help cover the $115,000 purchasing price, establishing his intention to purchase the building. Judge M. F. Edwards determined that within twenty days Adams must pay the purchase price ($114,000 in addition to the $1,000 paid prior to the suit) and 6% interest on the property.[71]

In 1926, work on the building began. The architect for the project was E.F. Red of Des Moines with Chris Rye and Son contracting the project. The estimate for the total remodeling cost was $30,000.[72] The Adams family intended to convert the bank quarters

Advertisement for City National Bank. Photograph Archive, digital file "CNB," Loomis Archives, MCPL.

[69] Leland Sage, *A History of Iowa* (Ames: Iowa State University Press, 1974), 253-254.

[70] *Polk's Mason City Directory,* (Kansas City: R.L. Polk and Co.) 1926.

[71] "Holds Instrument as Agreement to Purchase Building for $115,000," *Mason City Daily Times* 14 May 1926.

[72] "Remodeling Bank Building," *Mason City Globe Gazette* 31 December 1926; Chris Rye was the Mason City builder for a number of the Rock Glen residences and lived in a Prairie School home himself.

into retail space. To create more office space, the major alteration dropped the first floor to grade level and installed a new second floor between the top floor and the floor of the high banking space.[73] Single-paned glass storefronts separated by granite columns for multiple retail spaces replaced the solid brick façade of the bank building. To allow the second-floor installation, the stone horizontal belt course was lowered by eight brick courses. Standard wood, double-hung windows replaced the clerestory windows. The third-story windows, ornamental detailing and roof overhang remained unaltered, showing the building's original form and style. The interior space was entirely gutted and remodeled. Opening the single-story extension to the south of the bank to the street allowed additional retail space. The bank vault, tellers' windows, Bock statues, art-glass window, skylights and ornamental urns were either hidden from view or moved to other locations.[74]

Even before the project's completion, area businesses had already selected their spots. The United Cigar store and a clothing shop chose locations on the first floor. Second and third-floor office space quickly rented to the Farmer's Mutual Insurance Company, the Spencer Beauty Salon, the Northern Oil Company, the Prudential Insurance Company, a music service bureau, a barber, a local chiropractor, and an osteopath.[75]

The new and "improved" building was known as the "Weir Building. The local newspaper declared, "A somber and stern bank structure metamorphosed into a light, attractive, well-arranged store and office building."[76] According to the *Mason City Globe Gazette*, the remodeling "represents the culmination of a long-cherished dream of the Adams family." Mrs. Adams was the direct descendant of the 1870-1874 property owner, William Weir; thus it returned to the family after 52 years.[77]

Although the changes desecrated the aesthetic unity and proportions of Wright's building, they led to a commercial building that was economically viable and well-maintained until 2007 when it was purchased by Wright on the Park, Inc. to rehabilitate the entire bank-hotel building to its original architectural integrity.

City National Bank c. 1935. Photograph Archive, digital file "CNB," Loomis Archives, MCPL.

[73] Ibid.

[74] Dr. Robert E. McCoy, *Mason City Walking Tour Guide* (Mason City: Iowa: Larson Printing, 2003).

[75] "Remodeling of Weir Building Completed," *Mason City Globe Gazette* 2 March 1927.

[76] Ibid.

[77] "Old City National Bank Property, 'Lost' for 52 Years, Returns to Family," *Mason City Times Herald* 5 June 1926. "In 1870, William Weir became owner of the land on which the City National bank building stands." In 1874, under threat of litigation, he placed the title to the property with his friend H.C. Day to hold for him. Once the threat had passed, Day would not return the land; and when he died in 1903, he deeded it to his sister Hattie Ogden. Day lived alone in an attic room of the "little wooden building known as the 'Yellow Spot.'" Weir did try to regain the land when he sued Day in the late 1870s, but was defeated because he had transferred the land to Day "with fraudulent intent" to avoid losing it in a lawsuit. In 1906, Hattie Day Ogden filed suit against the Weir heirs, disputing again their claim. "Mason City is Happy," *Mason City Times-Herald* 25 May 1906.

Over its history, the first floor of the bank building hosted a variety of retailing endeavors, primarily clothing merchants. In 1926 Louis Goldman Clothier's occupied the main banking room; in 1927, the United Cigar Company held shop in the other storefront bay on the first floor. The long-lived business served Mason City until 1952. Jernegan Clothier maintained a business from 1927-1928 before being named National Klothiers. During the Depression years from 1931 to 1934, the second first-floor retail space sat vacant until Hub Clothiers, a men's clothing store, moved into it in 1934. Remodeling took place again in 1952 when Hub Clothiers expanded their retail space by removing the partition between the clothier and the area formerly occupied by the United Cigar Store. Hub Clothier remained in the space until 1973 when Leanna Nelson of Iowa City purchased the bank building from Willard Adams, the son of A. A. Adams, for $77,000.[78] In May of 1974, Van Duyn's clothing store opened after minor remodeling and occupied the bank building from 1974 to 1983. This

City National Bank, 2 June 1954. Photograph Archive, digital file "CNB," Loomis Archives, MCPL.

---

[78] "Weir Building is purchased for $77,000," *Mason City Globe Gazette* 18 December 1973. Mrs. Nelson's husband attended WOTP's October 2009 presentation in Iowa City, bringing photographs and his memories of the remodeling work he did on the upper floors of the bank building.

later became Eddie Quinn Clothing for six years. Through April 2008, the bank building served as the retail space for Moorman Clothiers. The Sara Building Partnership purchased the bank building from Leanna Nelson in 1983.[79] Wright on the Park, Inc., acquired the building in September 2007.

The upper floors of the bank building have had a variety of different occupants, primarily insurance and real estate offices. After the renovation of the bank building, the second and third-floor spaces quickly filled. On the second floor, insurance, chiropractic and real estate offices as well as a beauty shop operated. The third floor had seven rooms, all occupied by insurance agents. Long-standing renters on the second floor included the Pine Loan Company, located in the space from 1931 to the mid 40s. This company installed one of the first neon signs in Mason City.[80] Another long-standing occupant, optometrist Henry Knutson located in the space by 1940 and ran the practice until his son M.L. (LeRoy) Knutson took over. In 1985, the second-floor space again held a variety of occupants. One of the most long-standing renters was Hussey and Company, a fertilizer and chemical application equipment retailer which occupied many of the office spaces until 2008.

In 1948, KSMN Radio began broadcasting on March 1 from the third floor of the bank building. Under the management of Robert Carson, it added an FM station in 1961, broadening its listening audience. In the 1970s, KSMN moved to larger quarters.[81] The third-floor remained vacant until the 1980s when it hosted several businesses. McCoy and Co., a public accounting firm, stayed on the third floor from 1985 to 2005. After its formation, the non-profit organization WOTP operated offices in the bank building until it was the last occupant to move to allow rehabilitation to begin.

"A bank building of this type is usually either an undignified collapse between pseudo-classical temple and a one-horse office building, or it is the one with the other piled on top of it. The fenestration of the offices in this case was combined with the fenestration necessary to amply light the bank, (so) that of the whole window treatment a richly varied frieze was formed above to crown the massive unbroken wall surface below. The offices thus absorbed in the nature of the scheme and contributed to the dignity of the whole building instead of detracting from it.

"The building is what it is by virtue of its nature and has the solidity, dignity and completeness which ideals of this character alone can give to a building. The same stone and brick which built the outside built the inside. The interior fittings were designed in connection with the reinforced burglar proof vault altogether of permanent materials and of the same character as the walls so that the bank room and fittings are a unit. There is common sense in the handling of the various features of this building. There is such a thing as common sense in the art of architecture. What distinction the structure has is due, in a measure, to this extraordinary view.

"As any good thing artistically must have, the building as a whole has a marked, distinct individuality. This is due in large measure to the sane ideals behind its design, the common sense of its structure and somewhat to the feeling for proportion and the knowledge of architectural grammar possessed by its architect.

"It is an honest pioneer in a field where wasteful pretense and borrowed finery are used to characterize and give distinction to enterprises which are in themselves simple and dignified, if treated honestly on the merits."

"Prepared for this newspaper by the architect Frank Lloyd Wright"
From "City National Bank Moves to Its New Home," *Mason City Times* **5 November 1910. Other sections from the article are on pages 19, 20 and 28.**

---

[79] Throughout this section, the dates during which each business occupied the building are from *Polk's Mason City Directory* including the 1920, 1926, 1926-74, 1953, and 1975-1990 directories. "Expanding Store," *Mason City Globe Gazette* 15 April 1952, detailed the expansion completed by Hub Clothiers. Information on more recent moves provided by Wright on the Park, Inc.

[80] "Increase in Business Reported by Company Since Organized Here," unidentified newspaper article, *Prairie School Vol. 1*, Loomis Archives, MCPL.

[81] Vertical file, "The Communicator," Loomis Archives, MCPL.

Law Office and Retail Space

In the Larkin Building and the Unity Temple, the narrow waist between the two segments of each building contained the principal entrances used by everyone. The lawyers' north-facing entrance between the City National Bank and the Park Inn Hotel assumed similar importance in the recess between the sections. The entry staircase allowed client and public access to the second-floor law offices, the top-floor rental offices over the bank or the lower-level retail shops. The firm moved into its new office August 29, 1910. The *Mason City Times-Herald* congratulated them: "They have built a large legal business and their quarters will certainly give them a far better opportunity to take care of clients."[82]

Blythe, Markley, Rule and Smith continued to be successful in their new quarters. However, some time between 1916 and 1918, to be near one of their main clients, the Denison Brick and Tile Company, the firm moved their practice to the MBA building. Its construction began on December 24, 1915, with ex-President Howard Taft on hand to dedicate the new building June 6, 1917. The eight-story building occupied a "good and substantial site," the corner of State and Michigan Streets (now Delaware Avenue).[83] In 1948, Denison, who by then had acquired all 18 Mason City brickyards, bought the building, renaming it the Brick and Tile Building. In this location, the firm's partners continued to change over the years, but Blythe and Markley remained the senior members until their 1930s retirements. Arthur Rule also stayed a partner, as indicated in a 1929 sketchbook of prominent men in the community.[84] Even after their retirements, the firm maintained the name Blythe, Markley and Rule until 1953.[85]

Bank remodeling by the Adams family in 1926 added a clay tile wall dividing it from the law office space to facilitate separate ownership of the bank and hotel. The law office thus became accessible through either the hotel or the central waist.

Wright originally planned the first-floor level of the hotel east bay at 9 West State as a breakfast room, lunch room and bakery with the sky-lit room behind the lobby as the café, a more formal dining room. Actually, the east bay was first used as a billiard hall. According to a *Mason City Globe Gazette* article, new pool and billiard tables were advertised at 108 South Main in the first building south of the bank with "an entrance through the hotel on State Street."[86] The 1918 Sanborn Fire Insurance Map verifies that the east bay area served as the "Alexandria Billiard Parlor" with a connection through a doorway at the rear of the hotel's east bay."[87]

Solid wall planking in the law office, 1999. Archived Photographs, "Existing conditions 1999," Bergland and Cram Architects, Mason City, Iowa. (BCA)

[82] "Old Legal Firm in New Offices."

[83] "MBA Christmas," n.d., unidentified newspaper article from vertical file, "Bus. MBA," Loomis Archives, MCPL. "When it became established that tiling of Iowa's farms would increase the productivity, the demand for drain tile sky-rocketed to the point where Mason City became the world's largest producer of this product. The industry was dominated by the Denison-Keeler families" utilizing a 40-foot deposit of blue and yellow clay in the southwest part of the city. Centennial Edition, *Mason City Globe Gazette* 1 June 1953, p. 21.

[84] *Who's Who in Mason City Iowa*, local publication, 1929, Loomis Archives, MCPL.

[85] The firm's name last appears in *Polk's Mason City Directory*, 1953.

[86] Advertisement from the *Mason City Globe Gazette* 17 June 1910.

[87] 1924 Sanborn Fire Insurance Map" (Des Moines, IA: Sanborn Co., 1918).

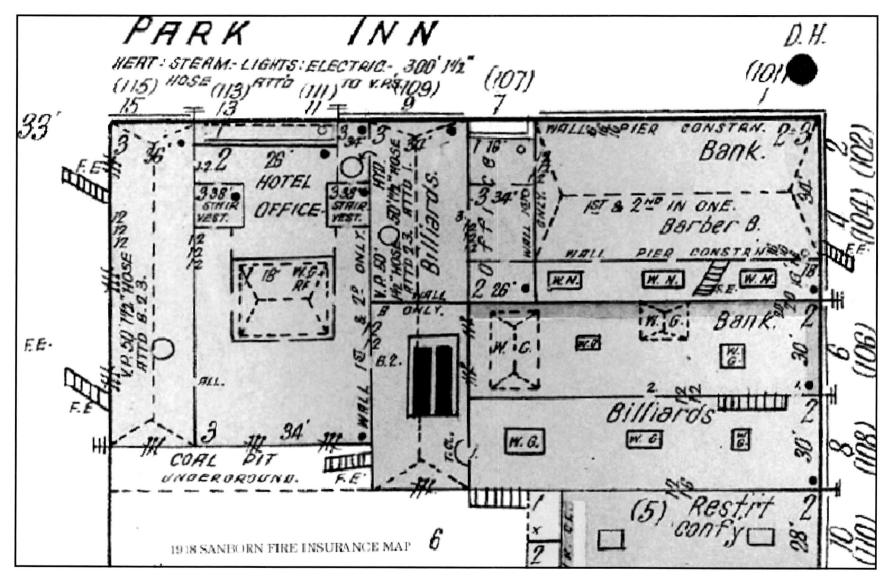

1918 Sanborn Fire Insurance Map. Note the entrance at the rear of 9 West State into 108 South Federal Avenue. Photograph Archive, digital file "Park Inn Hotel," Loomis Archives, MCPL.

By 1920, 9 W. State was no longer a billiard hall and the doorway between the two properties was removed. The space then served briefly as a hub for the Rediker Taxi Line in Mason City.[88] In 1924, the Red Ball Transportation Company moved from 6 North Washington to the first-floor space.[89] Helen Schultz, known as "Iowa's Bus Queen," operated the company. Although Mason City had a practical transportation system already in place with six railroads, Schultz took a chance and developed a successful bus transportation business. The bus line operated routes north and south from Des Moines to Minneapolis and east and west from Spirit Lake to Waterloo. The Red Ball Transportation Company ran routes until 1930, when Schultz sold the business to Edgar Zelle of the Jefferson Transportation Company for $200,000.[90]

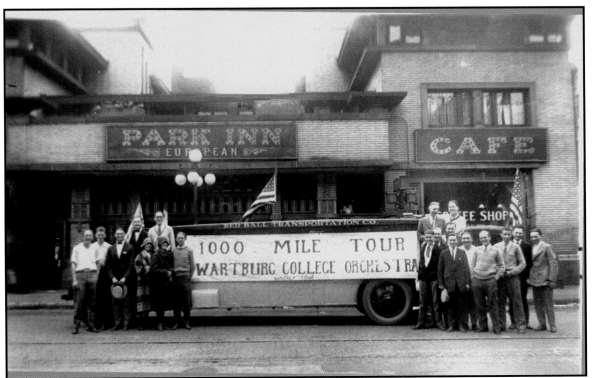

The Wartburg College Orchestra in a Red Ball Transportation bus outside of the Park Inn Hotel.
Photograph Archive, digital file "Red Ball," Loomis Archives, MCPL.

[88] *Polk's Mason City Directory*, 1920.
[89] *Polk's Mason City Directory*, 1927-1974.
[90] Margaret Walsh, *Making Connections* (Burlington, VT: Ashgate Publishing Company, 2000); *Polk's Mason City Directory*, 1927-1974.

Mutual Federal Savings & Loan Association and Bracken Insurance Agency occupied 9 W. State from 1933 to 1945.[91] Some time between 1933 and 1938, as evidenced by photographs, they added an entrance to allow clients to enter the space directly from the street.

The first floor served a variety of uses over the decades. A shoe repair shop took short-term occupancy in the east bay of the hotel in 1947. The next long-term resident of the space, the Tot and Teen shop sold children's clothing from 1953 to 1958. In 1960, the Thrift Plan Loan Company began offering services and stayed at that location until 1978. The Money Shop briefly occupied the space in 1980, but the space was vacant by 1983.[92] In 1991, Central Park Dentistry became the last occupant of 9 W. State, remaining open until 1995 when the business moved. After that, the space stayed vacant until rehabilitation.

The lower level variously held a barber shop, Fiala the Tailor and a salon. In 1927, T. A. Nyhus was listed at 9 ½ W State, the lower level of the east bay. He remained until 1933 when the Park Inn Beauty Shop owned by LaDonna Vanderveer entered the space. Jean's Beauty Salon occupied the space from 1938-1940.[93]

9 West State 1935-1939. Photograph Archive, digital file "CNB," Loomis Archives, MCPL.

[91] *Polk's Mason City Directory,* 1925-1940, 1927-1974.
[92] *Polk's Mason City Directory,* 1927-1974, 1975-1990.
[93] *Polk's Mason City Directory,* 1925-1940.

The Park Inn is a model whether in the domain of eatery or sleepery, or perhaps to be more correct – in cuisine and comfort. It is a marvelously well planned hostelry, every room of that sixty-one rooms but one being an outside room with art glass French windows, mahogany furniture, Cadillac tables, brass beds with box mattresses, lavatories with hot and cold water, luxurious bath rooms – everything new and sanitary and comfort wooing. . . [94]

Postcard of Park Inn Hotel, Bloom Bros. of Minneapolis, 1911. Photograph Archive, digital file "Park Inn Hotel," Loomis Archives, MCPL.

The local press raved over the Grand Opening of the Park Inn Hotel. In the most up-to-date "European" fashion of the time, most two rooms shared a bath while others had access to a bath off the hallway. In 1910, only the most expensive, lavish hotels offered private baths. However, sinks with hot and cold running water in each room afforded guests convenience. The ladies' parlor and gentlemen's lounge and mezzanine balcony between the front lobby and the café attracted attention as well and "earned generous praise from the public." The head clerk, Bert Watson, was heralded as a "gentleman of large experience . . . very popular with the traveling public.." [95]

Wright intended to create a warm and inviting space. A local reporter responded, ". . . with the quaint ventilated doors, the Flem- ish finish in hard pine with bungalow effect, in the architecture a guest feels that he is living in one of those delightful Craftsmen homes which is so restful because of its quiet and broad lines, harmonious proportions, and well selected tints of walls and ceilings. . . The 'elegant' café dining area serves only the 'finest cuisine with a European flair.'" [96] Eight courses with 14 plates gave the restaurant guests

---

[94] "New Park Inn is Ideal," *Mason City Globe Gazette* 10 September 1910. The reference to "sixty-one rooms" apparently refers to all of the rooms in the hotel instead of just guest rooms;

[95] "New Park Inn is Ideal."; "Head Clerk of the Park Inn," *Mason City Times* 10 September 1910.

[96] "New Park Inn is Ideal."

a variety of menu choices: a consommé royal soup, fillet of sole mornay, mignon à la pompadour, prime ribs of young beef, Yorkshire pudding, green beans au beurre, mashed potatoes, and a selection of desserts. The dining room boasted colored art-glass windows and mahogany furnishings in the Mission style. "The café is a sumptuous nook with a number of private compartments for small dinner parties leading from the main room all artistically furnished with the parti-colored art glass to give it the mellow tints by day and unique electric effects for brilliancy by night." On the opening evening, a small orchestra on the mezzanine balcony played for the guests during dinner, enhancing the hotel's elegance and richness.[97]

The Park Inn Hotel was the epitome of chic in its early days. The hotel prospered between 1910 and 1920 when it served as the premiere locale for fine dining and luxurious accommodations. Blythe and Markley co-owned the property with J.H. Sundell leasing the hotel and restaurant. An improvement to the building came in 1914 when Blythe installed a "smoke burner" to lessen the amount of emission from the coal furnaces. The purchase of the "Combustion Chamber and Fuel Saver," manufactured by William Galleway, followed complaints about the amount of smog produced by Mason City business and industry. Blythe, a proponent for improved air quality in the city, insisted other businesses follow his example and agree to reduce pollution.[98]

According to the Mason City directory, Bowers and Swanson managed the hotel as its popularity waned in the early 1920s when the rooms became dated.[99] The European style accommodations went out of vogue as patrons demanded more modern conveniences. In 1922, familiar competitor Charles Hanford McNider brought a new 250-room hotel three blocks to the north of the Park Inn.[100] The Park Inn faced a difficult time ahead.

Top: **Park Inn lobby looking toward the SW corner of the original café c. 1915. Note that the art glass ceiling appears to be present but not illuminated by its skylight and the mezzanine balcony has been removed. Wright's wood moldings are still present, but the walls have been wallpapered. The elevated ceiling that gave head room for the balcony remains.** *Above:* **Cigar counter detail, Photograph Archive, digital file "Park Inn Hotel," Loomis Archives, MCPL.**

[97] Ibid. [See Appendix B for information on the musicians.]
[98] "Smoke Burner is installed by Park Inn," *Mason City Times* 21 January 1914.
[99] *Polk's Mason City Directory*, 1925-1940.
[100] "Beginning to Take Shape," *Mason City Globe Gazette* 18 July 1920.

The Park Inn showing its patriotic colors. Photograph Archive, digital file "Park Inn Hotel," Loomis Archives, MCPL.

The plan for an upscale hotel, conceived in 1920, set a tentative opening date of April 1922.[101] The Hotel Hanford, designed by the architecture firm of Proudfoot, Bird and Rawson of Des Moines and contracted locally to the J.A. McDonald Construction company, rose eight stories. The structure had a steel skeletal frame with brick veneer and Bedford cut stone.[102] On its actual opening in June of 1922, the Hotel Hanford boasted 250 spacious rooms, complete with an ice-cold water supply and furnishings in American gum wood stained to look like black walnut. Private baths with softened hot water served each guest room. A large lobby invited guests in with marble wainscot in green and cream, a terrazzo floor and a green marble border. Modeled in the Georgian mode, the main dining room offered enough space for banquets served by a kitchen with the most modern of appliances.[103] The *Mason City Globe Gazette* claimed that "no city will have a finer hostelry and only one, Des Moines, will have one which exceeds the one here in size."[104]

Above: **Hotel Hanford interior, c. 1935.** *Top right:* **Hotel Hanford c. 1935. Photograph Archive, digital file "Hotel Hanford," Loomis Archives, MCPL.**

Due to the success of the Hanford Hotel, the Park Inn Hotel suffered loss of revenue. Bowers and Swanson left the establishment. Blythe and Markley then leased the property to G. D. Fletcher, who held it for only a year. In that time, business continued to decline. John Rich next managed the hotel and café in 1924, planning to remodel and update the property to help attract customers.[105] Little is said of the improvements of the spaces after one brief article on Rich. Changes, however, continued to be made: the mezzanine balcony over the desk was already absent by a 1915 lobby photo while the art-glass ceiling was removed before or at the time of a 1926 renovation.[106]

---

[101] "Beginning to Take Shape."

[102] "Mason City Now Best Hotel City," *Mason City Globe Gazette* 5 June 1922.

[103] "250 Rooms, all Conceivable comforts in Hanford Hotel," *Mason City Globe Gazette* 5 June 1922.

[104] Ibid.

[105] "New Manager Takes Over Park Inn Hotel," *Mason City Times* 24 January 1924.

[106] Dr. Robert McCoy, telephone interview, 4 June 2007, Mason City, Iowa.

Rich stayed only briefly at the hotel as Alfred Butters was listed as the manager of the Park Inn Hotel from 1925-1934. Butters ran the café from 1925-1926.[107] An advertisement in the Mason City directory indicated that the coffee shop underwent another change with Misters Harry Chu and Charles Wong taking over management of the coffee shop on May 24, 1927. The new business promised the finest foods, modern equipment and "Chinese dishes of all sorts."[108] The business under Chu and Wong lasted only until 1929 when the management of the restaurant reverted to Butters; it remained under his supervision until 1933.[109] In 1934 Blythe sold his half of the hotel and café to Markley, who leased it for one year to Blanch Pence with Joshua Gillam managing the coffee shop, but it changed hands soon .[110]

Top: Photograph of the Park Inn Hotel, c.1920. Above: Postcard of the hotel c. 1920. Photograph Archive, digital file "Park Inn Hotel," Loomis Archives, MCPL.

In 1935, S. M. Decker, a locally established restaurant operator, took over the management of the café. He installed updated equipment, fixtures and booths in the restaurant. The new facility also included a private dining room. Henkel Construction Company served as the general contractor with Seize Interior Fashions providing guidance for interior decorating and Federal Upholstering Company undertaking furnishing the space. The remodeled café opened to the public on Friday, June 18, 1935.[111] According to an advertisement, the restaurant, called the Park Inn Lounge Café, featured air conditioning and a "new luxurious atmosphere." Meals were served from 11 a.m. to 7 p.m.[112]

[107] *Polk's Mason City Directory*, 1925-1940.
[108] Advertisement for the Park Inn Coffee Shop, vertical file "Park Inn Hotel Archival Material," BCA.
[109] *Polk's Mason City Directory*, 1925-1940.
[110] Ibid.
[111] "Decker to Run Park Inn Café," *Mason City Globe Gazette* 31 July 1935.
[112] Ibid.

When Decker took over the restaurant in 1935, Mr. W. R. McBee leased the hotel. McBee had moved to Mason City in 1933 from Kansas City, where he operated another successful hotel. Under his supervision, the hotel underwent re-decorating. However, McBee died in an automobile accident in December of 1939. After his death, his wife Garnett operated the Park Inn Hotel until 1945.[113] J.E.E. Markley also died in 1939, leaving ownership of the property with his eldest daughter, Marion Markley Page.[114]

In 1945, Marion Page sold the property to Mr. and Mrs. Clarence Ellingson, who, with their family, operated the Park Inn Hotel and its restaurant. They came to Mason City from St. James, Minnesota, where they owned and operated the "64 Tavern" and the "313 Café." The Ellingsons made their family home in the southeast corners of the second and third floors in the seven rooms Wright had designated as house staff quarters.[115]

Perhaps the most serious threat to the building occurred under the Ellingson ownership. In April of 1946, *The Mason City Globe Gazette* reported, "Fire Checked In Park Inn; Held To Single Room." The three Iowa Falls men renting the room were out at the time, but another resident discovered smoke and unrolled the fire hose. Firemen found him overcome by smoke outside the room when they arrived. "Although all the furniture in the room and everything else inflammable was totally burned, the firemen had the blaze under control before the flames could break through the plaster into either the walls or the ceiling and the fire was restricted to one room." Firemen blamed the fire on a discarded cigarette.[116] Bank foreclosure on the building in 1972 ended its function as a hotel.[117]

1937 café in the Park Inn Hotel. Photograph Archive, digital file "Park Inn Hotel," Loomis Archives, MCPL.

[113] "Owner of Park Inn Killed in Auto Collision," unidentified newspaper article reproduced in *Prairie School, Vol. 1,* Loomis Archives, MCPL.

[114] Obituary index, "L-M," Loomis Archives, MCPL.

[115] An advertisement in the *Mason City Globe Gazette* announced the "Formal Opening of the newly remodeled Park Inn Lounge Café for Friday, June 18, C.I. Ellingson, Prop." (n.d.).

[116] "Fire Checked in Park Inn; Held to Single Room," *Mason City Globe Gazette* 2 April 1946. The resident regained consciousness and refused hospitalization.

[117] *Polk's Mason City Directory,* 1927-1974.

Above: Park Inn 1947. **The original hotel door and window glazing, curb and brass rail protecting the sub-grade-level windows and ornamental lanterns are still present.** *Top right:* **Cascade Room from the Ramona McCourt Scrapbook Collection.** *Lower right:* **Circular bar in the restaurant in the 1940s. Photograph Archives, file "Park Inn Hotel," Loomis Archives, MCPL.**

Forty years after the opening of the Park Inn Hotel, a letter to the editor appeared in the *Des Moines Register*. James Bethel told of his experience as an African American guest to the city. In 1950, as the nation was embroiled with racial tensions, James was sent on business to Mason City, where a room at an elegant hotel was reserved for him. However, due to his color the check-in clerk denied him a room; that clerk sent James to the "other" hotel across the square. The "other" hotel was the Park Inn. James wrote that he was extremely cautious about entering another establishment after the treatment he received at the previous hotel. Quickly, his fears were extinguished when the clerk "promptly and courteously" registered him as a guest. He said, "I was surprised and quite impressed with the 'business as usual' display of hospitality and I continued stopping at the Park Inn for all the years I traveled to Mason City thereafter." [118]

[118] "Recalls Acceptance at Park Inn," *Des Moines Sunday Register* 12 April 1970.

The editorial appeared in 1970, when the fate of the Park Inn was in question. After sixty years, severe deterioration affected it. Ellingson, challenged financially by the downturn in business speared by the Hotel Hanford's competition, owned the hotel for twenty-five years without making significant updates. By 1970, Mason City residents told visitors: "Don't stay there." A single room with a shared bath rented for only $3; a single room with a private shower was a bargain at $7; and for only $11, a guest could choose to stay in a double room with a private bath. Neon advertising and projecting signs promoted popular beers. The café-lounge circular bar and dance floor was "not an inviting space," and the lobby had become a penny arcade.[119] Without attention at the typical 20-30-year cycle, the roof leaked, encouraging mold growth. When the Ellingson's bank foreclosed, the Park Inn needed serious overhaul.

Coinciding with the hotel's deterioration, the 1970s brought the beginnings of community-wide interest in preservation. The Preservation Act of 1966 created the National Register of Historic Places with the opportunity for building owners to apply for federal funds to help rehabilitate and restore historically-significant structures. Following application in 1972 by a citizens' committee chaired by Shirley Crosman, the City National Bank, under the name the Adams Building, and Park Inn Hotel were added to the National Register of Historic Places, denoting their national value.[120] The city responded by calling out for someone to rehabilitate the building.

The city's request brought action in October of 1972. Richard Morel, businessman and owner of a successful jewelry store, intended to restore the hotel to its original appearance. He purchased the building on September 22, 1972, planning to adaptively reuse the second and third-floor space for apartments, leaving the first floor dedicated to offices and the basement as a restaurant.[121] Morel took some positive steps, including removing non-historic materials added during the many years of remodeling. He retained the original louvered doors and mahogany woodwork as well. The upper floors did become eighteen individual apartments, requiring the removal of some original wall partitions to enlarge the space. Apartment features such as stoves, refrigerators, sinks and cabinets were installed. Morel funded the project with a matching grant from the State Historical Society of Iowa, the state entity that oversees preservation work in Iowa.[122]

The rehabilitation succeeded for Morel initially. The lower-level office space and the "Frank Lloyd Wright Apartments" rented out quickly. From 1977 to 1989, the investment company Piper Jaffrey leased the east bay space. The Mason City Chamber of Commerce moved into the central bays and west bay of the first floor in 1974 and occupied it until 2001.[123]

In the effort to clean the masonry and terra cotta tiles in the Park Inn in 1973, Morel's restoration work included sandblasting the soft brick exterior and interior and using an acid-etching solution to clean the polychrome tiles. Although well-intentioned, the cleaning measures employed caused damage to the brick and terra cotta tiles. Morel's restoration work also failed to completely address the deterioration of the roofing or mold issues it engendered. The type of cleaning the Park Inn Hotel underwent in the rehabilitation was insensitive to the building materials and is not acceptable under the current preservation philosophy evidenced by the *Secretary of the Interior's Standards for the Treatment of Historic Properties*.[124]

---

[119] Stephen Seplow, "Time Cruel to Iowa Hotel By Frank Lloyd Wright," *Des Moines Sunday Register* 26 March 1970.

[120] National Park Service, U.S. Dept. of Interior, "National Register of Historic Places," 8 August 2009 <http://nrhp>; Otto Knauth, "History Unit Names Top Iowa Sites," *Des Moines Register* 9 January 1972. Crosman lived in one of the Prairie Style homes in Rock Glenn. The listing of the City National Bank as the "Adams Building" seems inconsistent, however, as the Adams family called it the Weir Building and it was locally known by that name .

[121] Park Inn Hotel Abstract, Community National Bank, Mason City, Iowa; James Owens, "Park Inn Hotel may be Restored," *Mason City Globe Gazette* 31 October 1972.

[122] Gary Grimmond, "Renovation at the Park Inn revealing," *Mason City Globe Gazette*, 12 May 1973.

[123] *Polk's Mason City Directory*, 1927-1974; 1975-1990; "Wise site selection," *Mason City Globe Gazette* 3 May 1974; John Skipper, "Park Inn Work Resumes," *Mason City Globe Gazette* 5 August 2003.

[124] McCoy.

Morel's undertaking was too great to be adequately funded by a single, private source. On February 1989, the bank foreclosed on his investment and took over the property. On October 23, the bank sold the Park Inn to local Clear Lake developer Les Nelson for $52,000.[125] Nelson continued to rent the apartments after updating furnishings. However, the condition of the Park Inn Hotel remained poor and the price of the apartments higher than their quality warranted. In 1990, gossip circulated around town that Nelson planned to sell the hotel to Phillip Broussard, a St. Paul, Minnesota, architect interested in investing in the property.[126] Nelson dispelled that rumor when he applied for a matching grant of $60,000 from the State Historical Resource Development Program for restoration work. With the once-failed attempt at rehabilitating the hotel into a successful business venture, the second grant allocation drew criticism.

An editorial in the *Globe Gazette* regarding the Frank Lloyd Wright property asked, "What function can support that form?" It expressed doubt that any "landlord could afford the $1 million to renovate the structure" as it would need to "generate $100,000 per year just to service the debt." As to the suggestion that the city buy the property, the editorial concluded, "Mason City can ill afford the acquisition. That leaves some benefactor to save the city's best example of Prairie School architecture. Who are they? Where are they? Absent private investment, the Park Hotel becomes a crumbling anachronism at worst; at best a lifeless museum memorializing a man who left his mark on the city 79 years ago."[127] The debate over the future of the Park Inn Hotel had begun.

Half a decade later, it seemed Nelson had not matched and therefore not received the state funds for the rehabilitation, and the structure continued to deteriorate. The leaking roof and resulting mold issues worsened. In 1996, David Christiansen, president of the River City Society for Historic Preservation, accused Nelson of "ignoring the situation and the significance of the structure on international levels," as highlighted by the Iowa Historic Preservation Alliance designation of the Park Inn Hotel as one of Iowa's "10 Most Endangered Properties."[128] The question of what to do with the hotel continued to generate controversy.

The terra cotta and polychrome tiles on the exterior of the hotel lost their brilliance when they were sandblasted in the 1970s. Archived photographs, "Existing conditions," BCA. (See page 79 for photo of the restored column.)

[125] Dyton Creative, 2007, "News," 22 May 2007 <http://www.wrightonthepark.org>.

[126] Steve McMahon, "Park Inn for sale? Maybe; maybe not," *Mason City Globe Gazette* 25 April 1990.

[127] "When Form and Function Diverge," *Mason City Globe Gazette* 16 October 1989.

[128] Baskins, Kevin, "Group makes historic hotel 'endangered,'" *Mason City Globe Gazette* January 1996.

Heartland Properties, Inc.

By 1999, the fate of the hotel remained unresolved. However, after three more years of deterioration, Nelson agreed to sell the property to the Frank Lloyd Wright Building Conservancy, the national organization dedicated to the preservation of Frank Lloyd Wright structures.[129] If the Conservancy purchased the building, it planned to place a historic preservation easement on the property and immediately sell it to a private Madison, Wisconsin, company, Heartland Properties, an unregulated subsidiary of Wisconsin Power and Light, which had approached the city as a possible lead investor in the Park Inn Hotel restoration. They first intended to rehabilitate it to ten condominiums, but they soon had to revise their plans to ten affordable apartments with commercial retail space on the first floor. An analysis done for the company outlined environmental hazards, estimating the entire adaptive reuse project at $1.7 million. With the city's help locating and funding a contiguous parking lot for the residents, Heartland hoped to ensure that the Park Inn Hotel survived.[130]

The last year in the century began as a hopeful one for those interested in saving the hotel. The Mason City Planning and Zoning Commission approved the establishment of a historic preservation overlay district for downtown, allowing the city to qualify as a "Certified Local Government" and making it eligible for federal and state funds.[131] In March, the Iowa House of Representatives approved a $200,000 allocation for the Park Inn Hotel. Sponsored by Republican representative Gary Blodgett of Clear Lake, the action provided funds specifically for use in rehabilitating the hotel roof.[132]

Forums, speakers, and editorials urged community support to raise funds for the project. Dr. Robert McCoy, retired orthopedic surgeon and Wright architecture expert, pleaded for the community to recognize the importance of the Park Inn Hotel: "If we fail to seize this opportunity to save this building now," McCoy wrote in a letter to the *Globe Gazette*, "it is unlikely that such a chance will ever be present again."[133]

Deteriorating roof with chimney requiring hoop-banding to prevent collapse. Archived photographs, "existing conditions 1999," BCA.

---

[129] "Park Project offers Mason City more than history," *Mason City Globe Gazette,* 2 March 1999. In the tentative agreement with the Conservancy, Nelson was to donate a portion of the appraised value to that non-profit group, which could lower the value with the Historic Conservation Easement and sell it to Heartland for the same price paid to Nelson.

[130] Kathie Obradovich, "Jail, Wright building 'endangered,'" *Mason City Globe Gazette* 21 January 1999.

[131] John Skipper, "Officials discuss historic designation," *Mason City Globe Gazette* 26 February 1999; "Park Inn project deserves backing of full community," *Mason City Globe Gazette* 25 March 1999.

[132] Kathie Obradovich and Bob Fenske, "House Approves funds for Park Inn," *Mason City Globe Gazette* 23 March 1999.

[133] Dr. Robert McCoy, "Mason City is at a turning point in Frank Lloyd Wright heritage," *Mason City Globe Gazette* 28 February 1999.

Advocates argued that the project would bring more tourists to town, help redevelop the depressed downtown, provide increased revenue to the city, and offer much needed affordable housing. Jon Lipman, past president of the Conservancy, described The Park Inn Hotel as "an untapped resource" that "other cities would kill to have."[134]

Even with all of the excitement and positive steps forward for the project, insurmountable obstacles began building by the summer of 1999. The initial estimate of $1.7 million to stabilize the property did not address the discovery of internal structural problems. In July of 1999, Heartland announced that it wanted to include the City National Bank in the plans for rehabilitation, raising the price tag from $1.7 million to $7.15 million.[135] The city council cringed at the new rehabilitation price tag but also at the city planner's conclusion that their financial commitment for parking would be $900,000 compared to Heartland's previously estimated $125,000. Responding to Heartland's conditions for purchasing the property, the steep project cost, the required parking space commitment by the city, the funding gap, and the use of the property for affordable housing, a councilman suggested that the city consider purchasing the property itself.[136]

The proposal changed the course of the Heartland plan, halting the project as the City Council debated the merits and other directions for the hotel rehabilitation. Councilman Ken Lee, who proposed purchasing the Park Inn, stated that it was taking Heartland too long to formulate a cohesive plan while the Park Inn continued to deteriorate. He suggested the city could purchase the property, use the $200,000 state grant to replace the roof, and then sell the hotel to Heartland.[137] The suggestion met varied opinions from the council and community. Dr. McCoy felt that the city should continue on its course, with Heartland taking the reins of the project.[138] Councilman Roger Bang proposed that the city lend money to a historical society or interested group so they could purchase and manage the property. In the midst of the discussion, Heartland Properties tried to clarify their position with the following statement: "What we want from the city is essentially two things – to commit to providing 10 parking spaces for residents of the apartments that will be built on the upper floors of the Park Inn and to work with us in finding and providing funding for the entire project." The spokesman for the company assured the city that Heartland preferred the acquisition of the City National Bank, but did not view it as completely necessary at that time. He urged the council not to undercut their plans.[139] Discussion on the correct course of action by the city continued for over two months. Eventually, in December of 1999, the council decided to approach the Mason City Foundation instead of going with the Heartland proposal.

Mason City Foundation

In the early days of 2000, a five-to-one city council vote decided that the Mason City Foundation (MCF) would indeed take over the rehabilitation of the Park Inn and do "museum quality" work.[140] Les Nelson sold the property to the city for $75,000; the city then sold it to the MCF interest free, payable in five years. The city, in order to continue receiving state funding, retained .5% of the ownership of the property. The agreement stipulated that all decisions must be approved by the Planning and Zoning Commission.[141]

[134] "Restore Park Inn, Wright expert says," *Mason City Globe Gazette* 3 March 1999.

[135] John Skipper, "Park Inn price tag: $7.2 M," *Mason City Globe Gazette* 15 October 1999.

[136] John Skipper, "City discusses purchase of Park Inn property," *Mason City Globe Gazette* 15 October 1999.

[137] John Skipper, "Council members disagree on Wright hotel purchase by city," *Mason City Globe Gazette* 18 October 1999.

[138] John Skipper, "City discusses purchase of Park Inn property."

[139] John Skipper, "Mix-up seen on Wright building," *Mason City Globe Gazette* 19 October 1999.

[140] John Skipper, "Foundation to purchase Park Inn Hotel," *Mason City Globe Gazette* 14 January 2000.

[141] Ibid.

The parties involved believed that the renovation would take no longer than five years to accomplish.[142] The Mason City Foundation began work on the property immediately. With the help of Bergland and Cram Architects, a local firm that worked previously with Heartland Properties on the architectural documents, the necessary clean-up and repairs began, starting with the top two floors. Mold and the deteriorated roof, deflecting as much as seven-and-a-half inches in some places, made that the primary concern.[143]

At this time, while the Park Inn Hotel received increased recognition of its significance and ongoing rehabilitation efforts, money came in to support the project. In early 2000, the Iowa State Legislative allocation of $200,000 arrived for the stabilization of the badly failing roof and re-roofing; the Farrer Charitable Foundation awarded an additional $5,000 grant for that purpose. Grants in 2000 also included a $7,500 Johanna Favrot grant from the National Trust for Historic Preservation to be used for a feasibility study to determine if and in what form the project could provide an economic return after completion. A $7,221 State of Iowa Historic Resource Enhancement and Preservation (REAP) grant addressed the same goal.[144]

As a result of the funding, roof work was completed and two teams of consultants came to Mason City: the architectural team of Nore' Winter, Kramer and Jessup of Boulder, Colorado, and economist Edward Starkie consultants from Portland, Oregon. The consultants' work considered the following use options: "Boutique Hotel and Restaurant"; Bed and Breakfast; Pensione Hotel (bathroom down the hall) and Restaurant; Two Mixed Use Combinations: Option 1) First floor - office, retail, gift shop (museum), restaurant and support spaces: Second floor - office suites; Third floor - condominiums. Option 2) First floor same as #1; Second and third floor, private residential condominiums.[145]

Above: **Herb Kennedy and Karl Griffith carefully removed non-historic elements in the ladies' parlor. Archived photographs, "artglass," BCA.** *Below:* **Original art-glass window revealed behind painted layer. WOTP, 9 August 2009 <http://www.wrightonthepark.org/galleries/1999>.**

---

[142] Ibid.

[143] John Skipper, "Work begins on top two floors," *Mason City Globe Gazette* 10 March 2000.

[144] Ann MacGregor, Executive Director, WOTP, June 2007 interview, Mason City, Iowa.

[145] The Park Inn Reuse Study, Final Draft: 5 March 2001, WOTP.

The consultants urged the MCF and city council not to limit the project but to "think big" for the nationally-significant structure because it was certain to bring a large amount of money to the community. In 2001, the MCF received the joint conclusions and written recommendations from the consultants. In the document, the consultants concluded that based on the models studied, the Park Inn would see a return on investment only if it were run as a twenty-two room hotel with restaurant and gift shop. Even though the rooms would rent for over $100 a night, expensive for Mason City, the cost was well in line with other specialized "boutique" hotels in Iowa.[146]

In April 2000, the Park Inn Hotel was designated a "Save America's Treasures" project. The designation announced the hotel as one of "the nation's irreplaceable historic and cultural treasures to be preserved for future generations." In September 2001, the MCF received a Save America's Treasures grant of $500,000 conditioned on an equal match to be secured for restoration of the hotel exterior including removing exterior fire escapes, re-pointing and cleaning all brick surfaces with replacement of damaged and missing bricks, applying new stucco above the third-story window sills, restoring exterior and interior roof drainage, tiling of roof ridges, and re-paving over the under-alley coal room. The funding also included provisions for structural engineering of the basement, operational casement windows, a skylight to protect the art-glass ceiling of the café dining area, reproduction of art glass, and restoration of five double French doors leading to the ladies' parlor balcony.[147]

Andersen Windows made a significant matching in-kind contribution of art-glass reproduction inserts for the 72 missing casement windows valued at $185,000 and custom window frames at cost. A 2004 $100,000 Historic Sites Preservation Grant through the State

Historical Society of Iowa assisted the work on the brick facade and the roof drainage system. The project start date was September 1, 2001.[148] With the match complete in 2004, the above projects began.

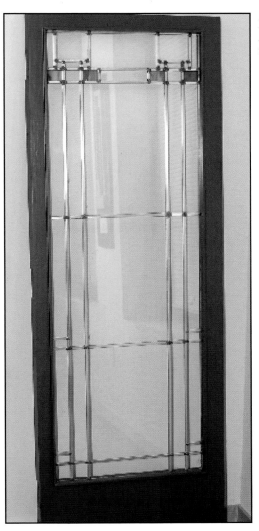

Ladies' parlor door, restored. Archived photographs, digital file, "artglass," BCA.

[146] Ibid.

[147] Tom Thoma, "Park Inn Hotel recognized by Save America's Treasures," *Mason City Globe Gazette* 4 May 2000.

[148] John Skipper, "Park Inn work resumes," *Mason City Globe Gazette* 8 May 2003.

Although the Mason City Foundation made more headway than any prior owner of the Park Inn Hotel, the amount of time required and the cost of repairs overwhelmed the group. The tight five-year time frame provided by the city council to fund and complete the project did not allow for unforeseen delays in the rehabilitation process. Furthermore, the foundation had taken over an unanticipated project not in their original mission: the promotion and preservation of the heritage of native son Meredith Willson of *Music Man* fame. The Mason City Chamber of Commerce placed pressure on the group to hire a project manager to organize and better direct the project. The chamber also recommended that a comprehensive plan for the City National Bank and Park Inn Hotel, downtown plaza and Central Park restoration be drawn-up by the city. As agreed in 2000, the MCF had five years to pay back the $75,000 and complete the project. As that deadline drew closer, the city council tabled action to extend the loan repayment period numerous times, much to the frustration of the foundation. Council members questioned the viability of the project.[149]

With all of these obstacles, the MCF formally withdrew its leadership position in the Park Inn rehabilitation project in February of 2005. David Vikturek, chief executive officer for the foundation, stated that the lack of trust from the council and the chamber of commerce were critical in the decision. He declared, "It is difficult to help in an environment where our help is not wanted. The foundation simply cannot serve effectively where the intentions, motives, committee members, process and project plans are not trusted by the council or the chamber." After the MCF stepped down, the Park Inn Hotel property reverted to the unprepared city.[150] The decision shocked many in the community and the council quickly convened to consider the future.

In an unusual move, the council followed a course of action which brought considerable discussion in the city and the preservation community. At the March 9 meeting, council members decided to advertise the Park Inn on eBay, the internet auction house. They did not intend to sell the hotel at auction, but rather to advertise it in a forum where the property might receive international attention and possible investors. The move brought many editorials and newspaper articles discussing the potentially negative message it sent about the nationally-significant property. The eBay option proved unsuccessful. Although the listing received many viewings, no actionable investment interest emerged.[151]

Wright on the Park, Inc.

Simultaneously, the city council announced it hoped interested groups that might purchase the property for restoration would come forward. That happened. Only days after the council called for community help, Robert "Chip" Kinsey III, a local attorney, facilitated a meeting at the request of Mayor Jean Marinos and Chamber of Commerce Executive Director Robin Anderson. According to the *Mason City Globe Gazette*, those attending concluded that a hotel entrepreneur was needed to operate the hotel but that the ownership should be held by a private, non-profit group. The group also agreed that there should be no deadline to the project, recognizing a major fault in the plan involving the MCF.[152] After a series of meetings with the community and among themselves, the citizen's group went before the city council to announce their interest in taking over the project. By the end of March 2005, Wright on the Park, Inc. (WOTP) had filed articles of incorporation with the Secretary of State's office. Board members included Jean Marinos, Peggy Bang, Robert Broshar, Hal Hofman, Martha Huntington, Herb Kennedy, Robert Kinsey III, Ann MacGregor, Robert Marolf, Robert McCoy, John Michel, D. Kendall Peter-

---

[149] John Skipper, "Chamber Board: Park Inn needs project manager," *Mason City Globe Gazette* 8 February 2005.

[150] John Skipper, "Park Inn left in limbo," *Mason City Globe Gazette* 12 February 2005.

[151] John Skipper, "Council seeks citizen input while studying eBay options," *Mason City Globe Gazette,* 9 March 2005.

[152] John Skipper, "Park Inn planning begins," *Mason City Globe Gazette* 12 March 2005.

sen, Gary Schmit, and Lee Weber. In May, the newly-formed group elected Peggy Bang, a visual arts instructor at North Iowa Area Community College, as president of the board of directors; Robert Kinsey III, attorney, as board vice-president; and Ann MacGregor, secretary. Somewhat later, MacGregor, retired founding executive director of Hospice of North Iowa, became executive director of WOTP. The group immediately began looking into funding opportunities and developing a business plan for the future of the hotel project. WOTP applied for non-profit, tax- exempt (501) (c) (3) status in September of 2005, receiving notification of approval in November of 2006. The City of Mason City officially transferred the Park Inn Hotel to WOTP in March 2006. In this agreement, the council imposed no timeline for completion of the project, nor did the group have to report to the council on its progress.[153]

When WOTP received the go-ahead from the city council, the board met in July 2005 with Audra Dye, Project Director of the Frank Lloyd Wright Building Conservancy; Royce Yeater, Midwest Director of the National Trust for Historic Preservation; and Bill Morrissey, past president of Historic Hotels of America and head of the hospitality corporation managing the St. Paul Hotel. WOTP quickly learned that any hotel based on a 1910 model could not survive in the twenty-first century. The consultants stressed that the public spaces should be accurately restored and that the hotel rooms must be of a size and quality to appeal to contemporary travelers.[154]

Interior rehabilitation undertaken by Wright on the Park. Pictured is the only remaining balustrade of the mezzanine balcony that ran from the east to the west side of the lobby between it and the café. Here it looks down into the west stairwell. The careful removal of non-historic features of the lobby was done by volunteers. Archived photographs, "taxcreditapp," BCA.

[153] MacGregor.
[154] Ibid.

Some of the board members made a series of visits to historic hotels in Iowa and Minnesota. The hotel managers frankly detailed their organizational structure and areas of success and failure. The board engaged hotel management consultants to address their issues in further depth. A document projecting operating criteria and pro-forma based on a 21 and a 27-room hotel emerged. A projected 27-room hotel would utilize six rooms on the top floor of the bank building in addition to the 21 rooms in the hotel building. It became clear that financial viability would be greatly increased by using the 27-room model. WOTP needed to own the bank portion of the building.[155]

Meanwhile, with project specific funding from grants, the organization focused on interior stabilization and repair as well as replacement of missing materials. The poor condition of the interior and exterior terra cotta tiles was addressed when Renaissance Restoration of Galena, Illinois, color matched tiles and used hand-mixing techniques to complete their restoration in August 2007.

Similarly, the job of restoring the original art-glass dining room ceiling began in earnest in 2006. About the time of the 1926 remodeling of the hotel lobby and café, the ceiling panels were removed because of the leaking frame. Subsequent photos show white painted wood panels in place of the art glass. The Blythe family decided to put a roof over the open second-story porch at the south end of their 1913 Griffin-designed Prairie School home in the Rock Crest/Rock Glenn development.[156] The question of what to do with the art-glass panels was resolved by storing them beneath the roof in a framework much like the one in the Park Inn.

As the home changed ownership, knowledge of the art glass heritage became lost. Likewise, no one knew what had become of the bank's art glass. Inspection of the City National Bank directors' and officers' roofs during repair brought the discovery of three multi-paned, stained-glass window panels still in place. Recognizing their similarity, Dr. Robert and Bonnie McCoy, the current homeowners, identified the randomly-arranged panels of a stained-glass ceiling in the Blythe house as those from the Park Inn. The McCoy's donated these to the rehabilitation project.[157]

One of 25 art-glass ceiling panels Wright designed for the café. Archived photographs, "artglass," BCA. The entire ensemble will be replaced into the café area as restoration nears completion. Photo by Dr. Robert McCoy.

[155] Kaler, Howard. "Park Inn Hotel Operating Criteria." May 2006. Wright on the Park Office, Mason City, Iowa.

[156] Blythe and Markley, as developers and owners of the building and thus the panels, had the right to decide how to preserve them.

[157] The McCoy's donation was made to the Frank Lloyd Wright Building Conservancy and earmarked for restoration work on the Park Inn Hotel.

Artisan John Larsen displays a restored art-glass ceiling panel. The panels will be put back into the café section of the hotel when rehabilitation is completed. Photo by Dr. Robert McCoy.

In order to verify the panels as those shown in the Park Inn drawings, Martha Huntington, Bergland and Cram project architect, worked with Troy Larsen who used computer-assisted design to arrange photos of each panel into their original configuration.

Troy's father, Clear Lake glass artisan John Larsen, restored the twenty-five art-glass ceiling panels, refurbishing the panels with a high level of sensitivity to the original glass. He deconstructed the panels, washed them in a non-abrasive bath and carefully reassembled them with new zinc cames.[158] Larsen reinforced caming that completely traversed panels with heavier bars on their topside to prevent bowing of the panels when displayed horizontally. Once the panels are installed, the bars should be invisible to the viewer below. When the largest panes contained fractures in three places or less, he repaired instead of replacing the components. Two previously replaced large panes had poorly matched glass. Larsen traveled to stained glass manufacturers in surrounding states to get the best possible match. In the spring of 2007, the completed three-foot-square panels were transferred to secure storage pending re-installation.

A new protective skylight to illuminate the art-glass ceiling was installed at the end of 2005. Its design promises to be more waterproof than the 1910 version.

---

[158] A "came" is a divider bar used between small pieces of glass to make a large glazing panel.

53

Clerestory grilles from the original City National Bank and Park Inn hotel in place as a fence at a Clear Lake residence. Fourteen of the original 25 grilles have been located, which leaves eleven to be reproduced. Archived photographs, "artglass," BCA.

Response to a Bergland and Cram published request elicited more discoveries. The glass panels for the six hotel dining room doors turned up in the garage of a Des Moines resident who donated them to the project. Fourteen of the cast grilles that guarded the bank's clerestory windows were in use as an ornamental fence between a Clear Lake residence and the lake. These owners, too, agreed to donate the grilles, which remain in secure storage awaiting restoration and re-installation at the appropriate time. These donations along with Andersen Windows' in-kind donation of reproductions of the missing art glass for the guest room windows and Larsen's restoration work marked significant progress in the quest for project authenticity.

In March 2006, WOTP received another funding boost from the Iowa Department of Cultural Affairs with the allocation of a $20,500 grant for architectural services. Around the same time, Wright on the Park, Inc., the River City Society for Historic Preservation and the Mason City Downtown Association applied for an "Iowa Great Place" designation. The Great Places program is a state sponsored program aimed at providing funding to communities, counties or areas in Iowa that show potential for cultural historic development. In October of 2006, Mason City received designation as an Iowa Great Place. After learning of the city's award, State Representative Bill Schickel said, "This has the potential to make Mason City's downtown a destination for not just the rest of the State of Iowa, but the rest of the country and indeed the world." [159]

When Heartland proposed expanding their project to include the bank as well as the hotel, the city found the projected cost overwhelming. But, as Dr. McCoy explained, " . . . the exterior restoration of the Park Inn Hotel cannot achieve a world-class level of quality until the exterior of the City Na-

tional Bank segment of the building has been restored to its original appearance in which its originally narrower, airy upper segment rests on its broader sold-brick base. It must re-achieve its original Wright proportions. . . ." Assisted with funding from the Iowa Great Places program and the Elizabeth Muse Norris Charitable Foundation, WOTP completed the purchase of the City National Bank on September 14, 2007. For the first time, the bank and hotel segments came under the same ownership. Ann MacGregor, WOTP Executive Director, commented, "The purchase of the City National Bank has always been a priority for the organization." She noted that the bank section of the structure was indeed a necessary element for the organization's plan for making the hotel economically feasible as well as for returning the building to its original design. [160]

Opposite: **Workers prepare to begin roof repairs. Jeff Heinz, 19 July 2000. Photo used with permission from the *Mason City Globe Gazette.* Above: Tuck pointing work on the hotel. Photo by Dr. Robert McCoy.**

---

[159] "Park Inn project gets $20,500 preservation grant," *Mason City Globe Gazette* 26 March 2006.

[160] John Skipper, "We're Great!" *Mason City Globe Gazette* 28 October 2006; Dr. Robert McCoy, 12 August 2009; Mason City, Iowa.

Bergland and Cram working drawings now show the third floor of the bank holding six additional hotel rooms for a total of 28. The drawings illustrate the intention to restore the structure to original proportions. Over the years, adding a second floor and subsequent exterior changes included removal of the clerestory grilles and windows and installation of lowered casement windows. This destroyed the natural banding which unified the bank and hotel sections and created an esthetically top-heavy look for half of the building. The intended design effect will return when the main banking room is restored to two stories in interior height with the windows returned to their original style. The multipurpose space will host banquets, receptions or conferences. [161]

In 2007, WOTP received a $200,000 legislative appropriation through Iowa's Department of Cultural Affairs Historic Site Preservation Grant program as well as other area foundation grants. The allotted funding has already been used for basement stabilization to strengthen support of the first floor and for reconstruction of the mezzanine balcony between the lobby and the café. It also allowed completion of the ladies' parlor balcony and soffit and for reproduction of the east stairway from the basement to the second floor. Also in the summer of 2007, the State Historical Society of Iowa and the United States Department of the Interior National Park Service accepted WOTP's applications for State and Federal Historic Rehabilitation Tax Credits. Their sale will provide additional funding for the project.

WOTP commissioned a market analysis to continue their appraisal of what the hotel's future might hold and to gather data to facilitate fund-raising efforts.[162] The board also began interviewing potential professional hoteliers to manage the operation. In August 2007,

56

At the 2009 annual meeting, WOTP Board President Jean Marinos presented awards to Karl Griffith, Bob Marolf and Mel Kennedy in recognition of the countless hours of volunteer time they have spent in the demolition of non-historic elements in The Historic Park Inn and City National Bank building. Photo by Pat Schultz.

the board of directors, assisted by a private consulting firm, investigated a capital campaign strategy. In addition, the Mason City Chamber of Commerce brought together interested parties from several organization to make an application for a Vision Iowa grant.

---

[61] Bergland and Cram Architects. The original plan called for 27 rooms, six in the bank building with two of the rooms in the hotel restored to Wright's original configuration. Revision of the plan restores only one room, allowing the addition of a twenty-eighth room.

[162] "Market Analysis," Hospitality Marketers International, Inc., Gregory R. Hanis, ISHC. Milwaukee, WI.

[163] The mission of Vision Iowa is "to organize, establish, oversee and provide approval of the administration of the Vision Iowa and Community Attractions & Tourism grant programs." State of Iowa: Governor's Office: Board Profile: Vision Iowa Board, 23 July 2009 <http://openup.iowa.gov/board/Vision+Iowa+Board/140>.

In addition to the Chamber of Commerce, the group included representatives from Wright on the Park, Inc., the Mason City Public Library Board, and the River City Society for Historical Preservation, the group planning an interpretive center next to the 1908 Wright-designed Stockman House-Museum, Wright's first building in the state. Vision Mason City supported The Historic Park Inn and City National Bank rehabilitation, a parking facility, an expanded Federal Avenue Streetscape, remodeling of the public library, and the interpretive center. They completed the application to Vision Iowa and, under the name Vision Mason City, conducted a campaign that raised the required matching dollars. The organizations involved, the Mason City Chamber of Commerce, the Mason City Council, and the County Board of Supervisors signed the final application. Vision Iowa responded with the offer of a contract allotting nine-million dollars to the Mason City projects.[164]

However, what seemed cause for celebration soon changed into another city-wide debate. Members of the city council expressed concern over the provisions of the contract, especially the part that would make the city financially liable for 21 years in case of the hotel project failure. Advocates and opponents crowded city council meetings; letters to the editor flourished on both sides of the issue; and a "Grass Roots" group formed to support acceptance of the Vision Iowa contract. Cerro Gordo supervisors wanted out, objecting to the clause that also held the county liable should the hotel fail.

After considerable delay and what seemed like the council's ultimate rejection of the plan, more proposals emerged. Finally, the city council approved contract revisions that also satisfied Vision Iowa. The changes included dropping some of the original projects proposed and shifting the library portion[165] of the funds to the city, which assumed continued responsibility for parking and streetscape work. The county's commitment was removed. The Interpretive Center funding remained part of the agreement and $8.2 million from the total grant was earmarked for The Historic Park Inn City and City National Bank rehabilitation. The Mason City Chamber of Commerce Foundation came forward as guarantor for the latter, replacing the city and county obligations, and Vision Iowa agreed to a shorter liability

Wright on the Park Executive Director Ann MacGregor handled the ribbon cutting for The Historic Park Inn construction project while program assistant Claudia Collier held the logo. Members of the Chamber of Commerce Ambassadors' group attended the event in March 2009. Wright on the Park, Mason City, Iowa.

period.[166]

One WOTP board member summed up the experience: "It was like holding one's breath for weeks to see what would happen. I think most of us on the board felt like we were riding an emotional rollercoaster!"[167]

---

[164] John Skipper, "Mason City hits $9 million Vision Iowa Jackpot," *Mason City Globe Gazette* 13 March 2008.

[165] A local bond issue approved the majority of the funds for remodeling the library. The original Vision Iowa application requested additional funding for the library above the amount provided by bonding. "Mason City bond issue passes," Radio Iowa, 7 Nov. 2007, 23 July 2009 <http://www.radioiowa.com/datesearch/index/cfm?searchterm=11%2FO7%F2007>.

[166] "Kudos to Council for Vision Iowa Vote," *Mason City Globe Gazette* 24 May 2009.

[167] Pat Schultz, 19 July 2009, Nora Springs, Iowa.

Restoration, Rehabilitation, and the Future

Securing Vision Iowa funding moved The Historic Park Inn Hotel and City National Bank project forward, but several pieces of the puzzle remained to fall into place. To coordinate these, Ron Fiscus of PlanScape Partners became project manager. His position fulfilled one of the conditions of the contract with project guarantor, the Mason City Chamber of Commerce Foundation. As the final funding for the eighteen-million-dollar undertaking, New Markets Tax Credits and contingency tax credits were secured through Iowa Business Growth Company and backing by area banks. Wright on the

Restoration work will return the building to its original exterior look. Tinted postcard, City National Bank and Park Inn Hotel c.1910. Photograph Archive, digital file "CNB," Loomis Archives, MCPL.

Park, Inc. also committed to raising an additional one-million dollars for a fund to enable on-going programming and maintenance of the building.

Bid letting on October 13, 2009, marked the next step forward. Originally, WOTP hoped for a grand opening to coincide with the one-hundred-year anniversary of the original opening on September 10, 1910. Postponement of the Vision Iowa contract finalization and other unanticipated delays made that unrealistic; consequently, revised plans predict completion in 1911.

Bids came in and contracts were issued. With "ground breaking" ceremonies on January 26, 2010, construction began on the restoration-rehabilitation project.

To say "construction began" is somewhat misleading. Volunteers contributed countless hours demolishing the non-historic elements of the building and hauling out debris. Over $2 million has gone to fulfilling the goals of individual grants. These include stabilization and re-roofing, cleaning and tuck pointing exterior walls, reconstructing the chimney, stabilizing a basement wall and replacing the kitchen floor. Contractors finished rough-framing the lost mezzanine balcony, installed a modern skylight above the café, and replaced the east stair and the missing stone banding and soffit of the ladies' parlor balcony. Restored art-glass ceiling panels await installation along with the art-glass clerestory lobby windows. Andersen Windows installed 72 casement windows with reproduction art-glass inserts.

Construction manager Gary Schmit of Henkel Construction Company and project architect Martha Huntington of Bergland and Cram Architects oversee the work.

The Secretary of Interior's Standards for the Treatment of Historic Properties sets the standards followed for the work on the building. The main lobby, former dining area, and ladies' parlor are to be substantially restored to their original configuration and condition. The corridors in the hotel as well as the law offices of the Markley-Blythe firm are also "public spaces," thus warranting restoration over rehabilitation. The lawyer's entrance between the two buildings will be restored to its original appearance. The hotel rooms, however, will be updated and enlarged to accommodate the modern guest. Each room will provide a private bath and modern amenities. In all, twenty-eight rooms have been proposed, utilizing space above the City National Bank as well as in the original hotel. The west bay of the first floor will return to its frequent past function as a restaurant offering meals to hotel guests and walk-in customers. In the basement, the gentlemen's lounge will potentially remain an open lounge for guests and meetings. A room off the lounge will contain a 1910 era pool table and exercise facilities are also planned. Meeting space has been proposed in the basement of the bank building. The furnace, utilities room, laundry, electrical service, housekeeping and employee lockers can be located in the rear of the hotel basement. [168]

While funding, design and construction issues took the forefront, WOTP continued other activities. Docents conducted scheduled tours while staff members frequently found themselves giving spontaneous ones to visitors. Events included the local showing of the film *The Last Wright*,[169] a documentary about the building; Iowa Public Television also aired the film. On August 9, 2009, an Associated Press article featured the project, resulting in encouragement from around the world. Iowa City's Design Ranch cosponsored an October program about WOTP and its work, highlighted by presentations by Bob McCoy on the history of the building and Martha Huntington on the restoration and renovation.

Program assistant Claudia Collier maintains an updated website (www.wrightonthepark.org). In addition, board member Peggy Bang heads the education committee, which sponsors events like the kids' summer architecture camp held at the MacNider Museum. In the future, WOTP anticipates sharing educational functions with the Mason City Architectural Interpretive Center operated by the staff of the Stockman House-Museum. Periodically, board members attend events hosted by the Frank Lloyd Wright Foundation and/or the Frank Lloyd Wright Building Conservancy to stay current on issues and trends.

"It is exciting beyond belief to see all of the hard work of so many individuals finally making this project a reality! We truly have a great team that has made this happen!"[170] commented Ann MacGregor as WOTP celebrated moving into the construction phase and began planning for a grand opening.

Far left: Docent Jim Collison conducts a tour of the hotel. **Left:** A tour group inspects the reconstructed mezzanine balcony. Photos by Pat Schultz.

[168] Bergland and Cram,

[169] *The Last Wright* was directed by Lucille Carra and produced by Lucille Carra and Garry McGee.

[170] MacGregor, 26 Jan. 2010.

Wright on the Park

Board of Directors
Ann MacGregor, Executive Director, Board Secretary
Jean Marinos, Board President
Robert S. Kinsey III, Board Vice-President
Dennis Reidel, Treasurer
Peggy Bang, Board Past-president, Education Committee Chair
Mark Frandle
Dr. Robert McCoy, Preservation Committee Chair
Melissa Schoneberg
Pat Schultz, Fund Raising Committee Chair
Lee Weber
John Wilson

Honorary Board Members

Norman W. Ray	William Allin Storrer	Jonathan Lipman
Chuck Offenburger	Richard Guy Wilson	

**With special thanks to the following retired members of the board
for their service to Wright on the Park**
Robert Broshar
Hal Hofman
Martha Huntington
Herb Kennedy
Jay Lala
Robert Marolf
John Michel
D. Kendall Petersen
Roger Peterson
Gary Schmit

Appendix A: City National Bank and Park Inn Hotel Floor Plans

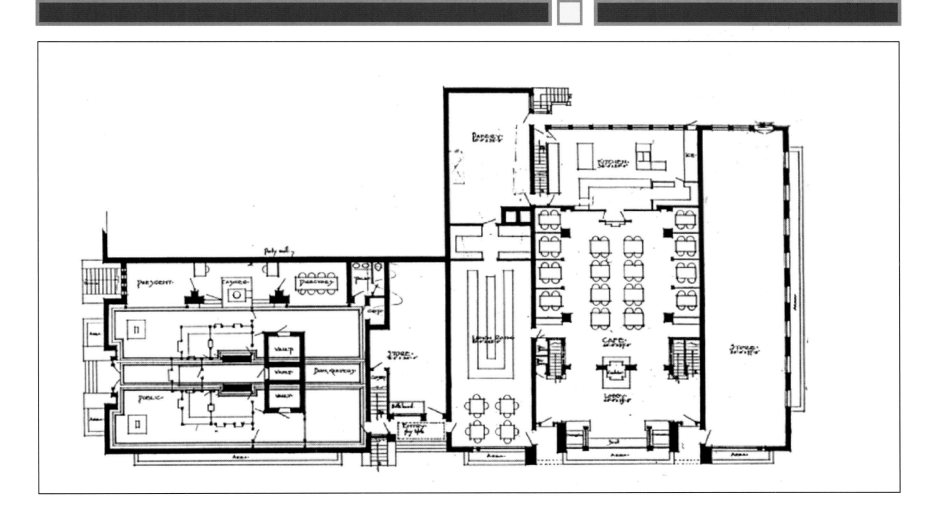

City National Bank and Park Inn Hotel first-floor plan. Frank Lloyd Wright monograph 1907-1913. A.D.A. EDITA, Tokyo, 1987, illustration 235.

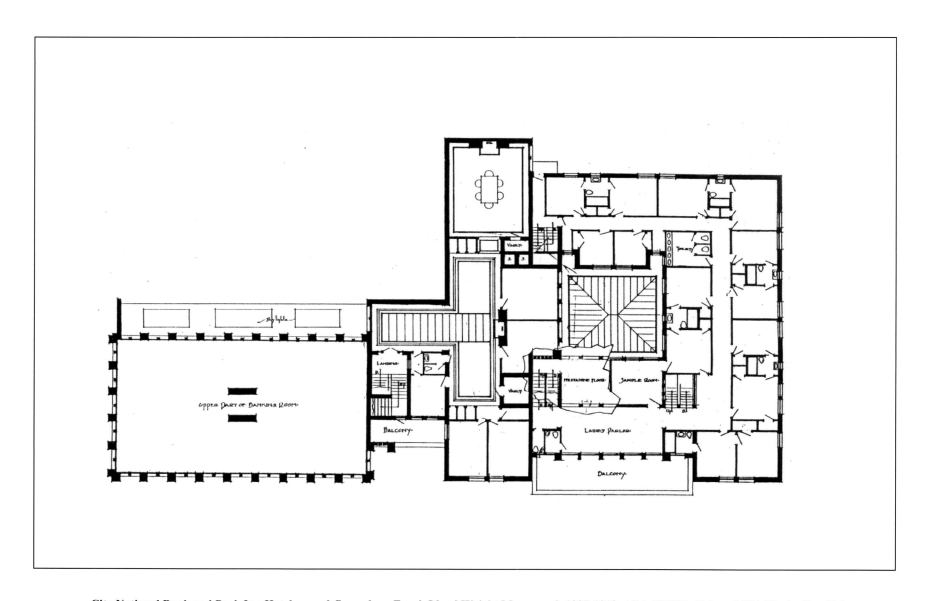

City National Bank and Park Inn Hotel second-floor plan. Frank Lloyd Wright Monograph 1907-1913. ADA EDITA, Tokyo. 1987, Illustration 234.

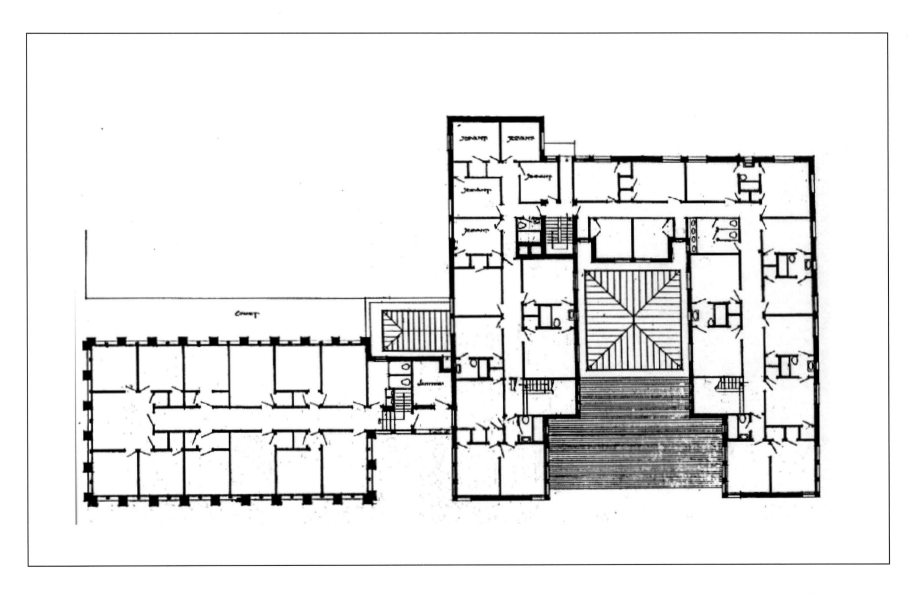

City National Bank and Park Inn Hotel third-floor plan. Frank Lloyd Wright Monograph 1907-1913. A,D.A. EDITA, Tokyo, 1987, Illustration 233.

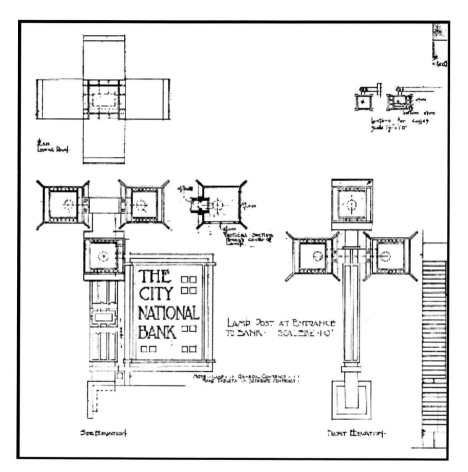

Wright's working drawings of the exterior light fixtures flanking the entrances of the bank and hotel. The Frank Lloyd Wright Foundation, Scottsdale, Arizona.

Detail of Prairie School light fixture beside east entrance of the Park Inn Hotel on West State Street. Photograph Archive, digital file "Park Inn Hotel," Loomis Archives, MCPL.

Appendix B: Additional Photographs

Left: Looking north up Federal Avenue from the block south of the City National Bank. The projecting eave of the City National Bank is seen immediately before the trees of Central Park. Buildings have been torn down immediately opposite the park to make way for the First National Bank, begun in the year after completion of Wright's City National Bank and Park Inn Hotel. Photograph Archive, digital file "Collection of Photographer Walter Burton Wright," MCPL. *Below:* State Street streetscape looking east, c. 1913. The Park Inn Hotel is on the right with Charles McNider's First National Bank in the left background. Photograph Archive, digital file "State Street from West," Loomis Archives, MCPL.

Above: North Federal streetscape, looking south. City National Bank is to the right, behind the trees of Central Park. Photograph Archive, digital file, "Postcard Collection," digital file "CNB," Loomis Archives, MCPL.

Right: Armistice gathering outside City National Bank, 11 November 1917. Photograph Archive, digital file, "CNB," Loomis Archives, MCPL.

Above: Federal Avenue streetscape. City National Bank Building, extreme right, February 1935. Photograph Archive, digital file "Safford Lock Collection," Loomis Archives, MCPL.

Right: City National Bank, c. 1910, Photograph Archive, digital file "CNB," Loomis Archives, MCPL.

Tinted photo, State Street looking west. The taller Times Newspaper Building is seen just behind The Park Inn. The photo, from 1954, shows the considerable changes to the exterior of the bank. Photograph Archive, digital file "Safford Lock Collection," Loomis Archives, MCPL.

Park Inn Hotel memories

Ramona Buffington McCourt, 2008

My mother, Hazel Buffington, worked at the Park Inn Hotel as a desk clerk during WW II. She started there a short time before Mr. Clarence Ellingson took over. She worked there for fifteen years or more.

Each one of the five of us Buffington children worked at the Park Inn at one time or another at various jobs.

My sister Phyllis worked for two days in the café—she was very shy and quickly found it wasn't her type of work . My sister Norma worked for a short time during the summer of 1950 as a waitress. She quit because she took the customer's complaints about how their eggs were cooked, etc., too personally. Plus she found some of the fresh remarks made by some of the male customers hard to deal with.

My time as a waitress in the café began the summer of 1950 when I was 15 years old. There were also booths and tables in the bar area where people ate. I worked in the café until school began in 1953.

My youngest sister worked in the coat and hat check room in 1955 for about two weeks — I believe it was in the lobby area as people went into the bar.

My brother Marlyn (at age 14 in 1954) worked at various jobs—washing dishes, janitor work and as fry cook . . . He remembers cooking a steak for Dizzy Gillespie. After the third attempt to get it cooked to Gillespie's liking, he sent it out to be served and said he'd better eat it this time because he wasn't going to cook it again! He also remembers cleaning out the urinal in the basement. It was one long one and didn't have any stalls.

Above: Interior view of the Park Inn restaurant at a time when it was in the west bay. Through the doorway the view is into the lobby with its cigar stand and the west stairway. Photograph Archive, digital file, "Safford Lock Collection," Loomis Archives, MCPL. *Opposite page:* Uncle Blockaway Carnival outside the City National Bank and Park Inn Hotel, July 1943. Photograph Archive, digital file "Park Inn Hotel," Loomis Archives, MCPL.

The Park Inn Hotel north façade facing Central Park.   The photo gives an excellent view of the hotel entrance into the lobby area, the Wright-designed light fixtures, and the ladies' balcony with its glass doors and urns. Original hotel room windows are on the right second and third floors while the windows to the law offices are on the left. Also illustrated are Wright's unique roof design and the colored tile columns on the exterior under the balcony. *Western Architect,* December, 1911, from Photograph Archive, digital file "Park Inn Hotel," Loomis Archives, MCPL.

North side of the City National Bank and Park Inn Hotel Building, 2002. Ninety-two years after its completion, the hotel section of the building shows little fundamental change in design while the bank's alterations are striking. The lowering of the windows to accommodate a second floor and the addition of display windows for retail stores on the first floor made that section appear top heavy compared to the original design, detracting from the unity Wright intended for the two parts of the building. Archived photographs, "existing conditions, 2002," BCA.

Top left: A side view of the ornamental urns on the ladies' balcony effectively shows the size of the pieces. *Left:* After one of its remodels, the Park Inn Hotel was again open for business. *Above:* Exterior of the Park Inn Hotel shows details of the art-glass windows. Archived Photos, "Park Inn Hotel," BCA. *Opposite page:* Photos of the Bock "Mercury" statue now in the Mason City Public Library by Katherine Haun, 10 July 2007. This statue was used as a model to reproduce the four statues for the bank building.

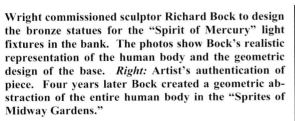

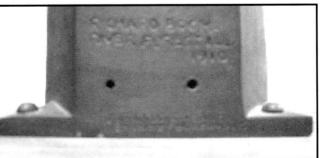

Wright commissioned sculptor Richard Bock to design the bronze statues for the "Spirit of Mercury" light fixtures in the bank. The photos show Bock's realistic representation of the human body and the geometric design of the base. *Right:* Artist's authentication of piece. Four years later Bock created a geometric abstraction of the entire human body in the "Sprites of Midway Gardens."

Park Inn Hotel memories . . .

From Art Fischbeck interview with Dewey Smith
Mason City, Iowa, August, 1998

I'd been familiar with the Park Inn Hotel for years because that's where all the musicians that ever hit this town ended up at night. And the guy that ran the hotel was a fellow by the name of Wallaby, Wellaby?

There were always musicians hanging around that they (band directors) could visit with to find out if somebody was available or not.

Lawrence Welk used to work out of the Park Inn here in Mason City occasionally. He didn't play there; that's where he'd pick up his band members before they'd go out on an engagement.

And then Bobby Griggs . . . that's where he always used to pick up his musicians. Just a gathering spot where you'd stop to pick them up before you played a dance. Then afterwards, you'd come home, stop there, and go in and have lunch. That's where everyone came, rather than running around the country picking them up.

Above: John Kopecky with his violin, which he played as a part of the Gates Orchestra.

The elegance of the 1910 Park Inn Hotel and its lobby and dining room is reflected in the Gates Orchestra members' attire. Advertisements for the hotel list the Gates Orchestra (also called The Imperial Orchestra) as an attraction. According to his daughter, Mildred (Millie) Thomsen, John Kopecky and this group entertained Park Inn Hotel guests frequently from 1910 to about 1915. They played for area dances and events as well as at the theatres. John later moved from Mason City to Clear Lake; he was the founder of the Garner, Clear Lake, and Ventura high school bands. *Opposite:* The Gates Orchestra including Bob Gates, harp; John Kopecky, violin; Tom Wells, clarinet; and Earl Hunt, drums. "John Kopecky Collection," Clear Lake Public Library, Clear Lake, Iowa, with thanks to H. Milton Duesenberg for scans. Kopecky photos reproduced with permission, Mildred Kopecky Thomsen, Clear Lake, Iowa.

Gates Orchestra advertising postcard. Kopecky collection, Clear Lake Public Library, Clear Lake, Iowa. *Right:* Park Inn Hotel postcard, 1930s, advertising the amenities of the remodeled "New Park Inn Hotel." Photograph Archive, digital file "Park Inn," Loomis Archives, MCPL.

Above: One of the original louvered doors leading from a hotel room into the hallway. *Right:* Troy Larsen's digital image of the 25 art-glass panels as they originally graced the Park Inn Hotel's Café. Troy, whose father John restored the panels, worked from individual photos taken by Dr. Robert McCoy. Removed from the hotel in about 1926 and stored for over 80 years in the Prairie School home of James Blythe, one of the hotel's two developers, the panels were given to the Frank Lloyd Wright Building Conservancy in 2000-2001. Dr. McCoy, who owns the Blyth home along with his wife Bonnie, said, "They were given in the hope that one day the hotel might be restored to the point that the glass ceiling could appropriately take its original place there. Now that day appears to be dawning."

Above: Workers nearing completion of the skylight framing over the hotel dining area. Once the restoration-rehabilitation of the building is finished, the restored original art - glass panels will bring light into the room reflected through their colors. Photo by Dr. Robert McCoy.

Left: Art glass in the middle French doors leading from the ladies' parlor onto the balcony overlooking Central Park. *Above:* The ladies' parlor awaiting restoration work. Photos by Dr. Robert McCoy.

"A resource to liberate this new sense of interior space as reality is this new qualification called glass: a super-material qualified to qualify us; qualify us not only to escape from the prettified cavern of our present domestic life as also from the cave of our past, but competent actually to awaken in us the desire for such far-reaching simplicities of life as we may see in the clear countenance of nature." Frank Lloyd Wright, *An Autobiography* (New York: Duell, Sloan and Pearce, 1943) p. 339. Photo: Wright-designed art-glass ceiling panels in the home of Dr. Robert and Bonnie McCoy. Photo by Dr. Robert McCoy.

Left: Restored column shows the improvement in the brick work and the terra cotta and polychrome tiles. *Above:* Wright on the Park, Inc. Executive Director Ann MacGregor and volunteer Bob Marolf stand under a new beam used in the reconstruction of the mezzanine balcony in the hotel lobby.

Bibliography

Primary Sources

Literature

Architectural plans. Bergland and Cram Architects, Mason City, Iowa.

Ausgeführte Bauten und Entwürfe von Frank Lloyd Wright. Berlin: Ernest Wasmuth, 1911.

      (Some confusion exists over the publication date of the Wasmuth Portfolio. Two early editions were printed. The first is often listed as 1910; the second as 1911. Some sources date both as 1911. Over the years, it has been reprinted numerous times.)

Blythe, James obituary. Obituary Index, "B," Lee P. Loomis Archives, Mason City, Iowa.

Hospitality Marketers International, Inc. Gregory R. Harris, ISHC. Milwaukee, WI.

Iowa Official Register, 1907-1908.

Kaler, Howard. "Park Inn Hotel Operating Criteria." May 2006. Wright on the Park Office, Mason City, Iowa.

"Markley and M.C.," newspaper article, "Markley Family Scrapbook," Lee P. Loomis Archives, Mason City, Iowa.

Markley, James obituary. Obituary index, "L-M," Lee P. Loomis Archives, Mason City, Iowa.

Mason City and Cerro Gordo County Directory. Dubuque: Telegraph Herald Printing, 1908.

McCourt, Ramona Buffington. Personal memoir. Mason City, Iowa, 2008.

National Park Service. U.S. Department of the Interior. "National Register of Historic Places." 8 August 2009. <http://www.nrhp>.

Park Inn Hotel Abstract, Community National Bank security deposit box, Mason City, Iowa.

"1918 Sanborn Fire Insurance Map." Des Moines, IA: Sanborn Co., 1918.

"1924 Sanborn Fire Insurance Map." Des Moines, IA: Sanborn Co., 1924.

Polk's Mason City Directory. Kansas City, MO: R.L. Polk and Co., 1920.

Polk's Mason City Directory. Kansas City, MO: R.L. Polk Co., 1926.

Polk's Mason City Directory. Kansas City, MO: R.L Polk and Co., 1927-1974.

Polk's Mason City Directory. Kansas City, MO: RL Polk and Co., 1953.

Polk's Mason City Directory. Kansas City, MO: RL Polk and Co., 1975-1990.

Wright, Frank Lloyd. "City National Bank of Mason City." *Western Architect.* 27:105. December 1911.

Wright, Frank Lloyd. *An Autobiography.* New York: Duell, Sloan and Pearce, 1943.

Interviews:

MacGregor, Ann, Wright on the Park Executive Director. Interview 25 July 2009.

Schultz, Pat, Wright on the Park Board Member. Interview 19 July 2009. Nora Springs, Iowa.

Smith, Dewey. Interviewed by Art Fischbeck, 8 August 2008, Mason City, Iowa.

Newspaper Articles (Arranged by Date)

"Mason City is Happy." Mason *City Times-Herald.* 14 January 1907.

"The Annual Meeting." *Mason City Globe Gazette.* 14 January 1908.

"Plan for a New Bank." unidentified newspaper article 25 September 1908, reproduced in *Prairie School Vol. 1.* Lee P. Loomis Archives, Mason City Public Library, Mason City, Iowa

"City Bank Building Co. Incorporated." *Mason City Times-Herald.* 22 October 1908.

"City National will build April first." *Mason City Times-Herald.* 22 January 1909.

"The Old Yellow Spot Corner Will Soon Change." *Mason City Times-Herald.* 6 March 1909.

"The Man Who Named The Yellow Spot." unidentified article. 6 March 1909. reproduced in *Prairie School, Vol. I,* Lee P. Loomis Archives, Mason City Public Library, Mason City, Iowa

"Yellow Spot Corner Clear by April 1st." *Mason City Times-Herald.* 22 March 1909.

"Bank Plans Here." *Mason City Globe Gazette.* 31 March 1909.

"Why call it Yellow Spot?" *Mason City Times-Herald.* 3 April 1909.

"First Things in Mason City." *Mason City Times-Herald.* 5 April 1909.

"Unsanitary Spot Exposed." *Mason City Globe Gazette.* 31 April 1909.

Advertisement from the *Mason City Globe Gazette.* 17 June 1910.

"Old Legal Firm in New Offices." *Mason City Times.* 29 August 1910.

"New Park Inn is Ideal." *Mason City Globe Gazette.* 10 September 1910.

"The Eloping Architect Known Here." Unidentified newspaper. 9 November, 1910. Lee P. Loomis Archives, Mason City Public Library, Mason City, Iowa.

"Head Clerk of the Park Inn." *Mason City Times.* 10 September 1910.

"City National Bank Moves to its New Home." 9 November 1910. Newspaper article reproduced in *Prairie School, Vol I.* Lee P. Loomis Archives. Mason City Public Library, Mason City, Iowa.

"Canned Cook Steals Ham from Hotel." *Mason City Times.* 25 August 1913.

"Smoke Burner is installed by Park Inn." *Mason City Times.* 21 January 1914.

"Stock in National Bank Building Watered." *Mason City Times* 30 May 1914.

"Providing Bank Protection." 5 September 1917. Newspaper article reproduced in *Prairie School, Vol. I.* Lee P. Loomis Archives, Mason City Public Library, Mason City, Iowa.

"City National Remodeled its Banking Rooms." *Mason City Globe Gazette.* 31 December 1917.

"Mr. Blythe's Public Career." *Mason City Globe Gazette.* 17 May 1920.

"Beginning to Take Shape." *Mason City Globe Gazette.* 18 July 1920.

"2 Banks to merge coming Saturday." *Mason City Globe Gazette.* 15 February 1921, 5.

"Mason City Now Best Hotel City." *Mason City Globe Gazette.* 5 June 1922.

"250 Rooms, all Conceivable comforts in Hanford Hotel." *Mason City Globe Gazette.* 5 June 1922.

"New Manager Takes Over Park Inn Hotel." *Mason City Times.* 24 January 1924.

"Holds Instrument as Agreement to Purchase Building for $115,000." *Mason City Daily Times.* 14 May 1926.

"Old City National Bank Property, 'Lost' for 52 Years, Returns to Family." *Mason City Globe Gazette and Daily Times.* 5 June 1926.

"Remodeling Bank Building." *Mason City Daily Globe Gazette.* 31 December 1926.

"Remodeling of Weir Building Completed." *Mason City Globe Gazette.* 2 March 1927.

"Meet James Blythe." *Mason City Globe Gazette.* 19 November 1927.

"Increase in Business Reported by Company Since Organized Here." Newspaper article reproduced in *Prairie School , Vol. I.* Lee P. Loomis Archives.

"MBA Christmas," n.d. Newspaper article from vertical file, "Bus. MBA," Lee P. Loomis Archives, Mason City, Iowa.

"Decker to Run Park Inn Café." *Mason City Globe Gazette.* 31 July 1935.

"Owner of Park Inn Killed in Auto Collision." unidentified newspaper article reproduced in *Prairie School, Vol. I.* Lee P. Loomis Archives. Mason City, Iowa.

"Fire Checked in Park Inn; Held to Single Room." *Mason City Globe Gazette.* 4 February 1946.

"Expanding Store." *Mason City Globe Gazette.* 15 April 1952.

Centennial Edition. *Mason City Globe Gazette.* 1 June 1953.

"Frank Lloyd Wright Designed Homes Here." *Mason City Globe Gazette.* April 1959.

Seplow, Steven. "Recalls Acceptance at Park Inn." *Des Moines Sunday Register.* 12 April 1970.

Knauth, Otto. "History Unit Names Top Iowa Sites." *Des Moines Register. 9 January 1972.*

Owens, James. "Park Inn Hotel may be Restored." *Mason City Globe Gazette.* 31 October 1972.

Grimmond, Gary. "Renovation at the Park Inn revealing." *Mason City Globe Gazette.* 12 May 1973.

"Weir Building is purchased for $77,000." *Mason City Globe Gazette.* 18 December 1973.

"Wise Site Selection." *Mason City Globe Gazette.* 5 March 1974.

"When Form and Function Diverge." *Mason City Globe Gazette.* 16 October 1989.

McMahon, Steve. "Park Inn for sale? Maybe; maybe not." *Mason City Globe Gazette.* 25 April 1990.

Baskins, Kevin. "Group makes historic hotel 'endangered.'" *Mason City Globe Gazette.* January 1996.

Obradovich, Kathie. "Jail, Wright building 'endangered.'" *Mason City Globe Gazette.* 21 January 1999.

Skipper, John. "Officials discuss historic designation." *Mason City Globe Gazette.* 26 February 1999.

McCoy, Robert. "Mason City is at a turning point in Frank Lloyd Wright heritage." *Mason City Globe Gazette.* 28 February 1999.

"Park Project offers Mason City more than history." *Mason City Globe Gazette.* 2 March 1999.

Skipper, John. "Restore Park Inn, Wright expert says." *Mason City Globe Gazette.* 3 March 1999.

Obradovich, Kathie and Bob Fenske. "House Approves funds for Park Inn." *Mason City Globe Gazette.* 23 March 1999.

"Park Inn project deserves backing of full community." *Mason City Globe Gazette.* 25 March 1999.

Skipper, John. "Park Inn presents building challenges." *Mason City Globe Gazette.* 15 April 1999.

Skipper, John. "Park Inn price tag: $7.2 M." *Mason City Globe Gazette.* 29 September 1999.

Skipper, John. "City discusses purchase of Park Inn property." *Mason City Globe Gazette.* 15 October 1999.

Skipper, John. "Council members disagree on Wright hotel purchase by city." *Mason City Globe Gazette.* 18 October 1999.

Skipper, John. "Mix-up seen on Wright building." *Mason City Globe Gazette.* 19 October 1999.

Skipper, John Skipper. "Foundation to purchase Park Inn Hotel." *Mason City Globe Gazette.* 14 January 2000.

Skipper, John. "Work begins on top two floors." *Mason City Globe Gazette.* 10 March 2000.

Thoma, Tom. "Park Inn Hotel recognized by Save America's Treasures." *Mason City Globe Gazette.* 4 May 2000.

Thoma, Tom. "Park Inn hailed as treasure." *Mason City Globe Gazette.* 5 May 2000.

Nicklay, Deb. "Park Inn roof work finds underlying damage is severe." *Mason City Globe Gazette.* 15 August 2000.

"Park Inn Hotel investment will pay big dividends." *Mason City Globe Gazette.* 12 December 2000.

"Restoring hotel to original use is best choice." *Mason City Globe Gazette.* 13 March 2001.

Skipper, John. "Park Inn project gets a $500,000 boost." *Mason City Globe Gazette.* 8 September 2001.

Skipper, John. "Chamber board: Park Inn needs project manager." *Mason City Globe Gazette.* 8 February 2005.

Skipper, John. "Park Inn left in limbo." *Mason City Globe Gazette.* 12 February 2005.

Skipper, John. "Park Inn will get extension." *Mason City Globe Gazette*, n.d. Vertical file, "2005," Wright on the Park office, Mason City, Iowa.

McCoy, Robert. "Park Inn: Save it or lose it." *Mason City Globe Gazette.* 2 March 2005.

Skipper, John. "Council seeks citizen input while studying eBay option." *Mason City Globe Gazette.* 9 March 2005.

Moore, Mike. "Park Inn on eBay a 'big deal.'" *Mason City Globe Gazette.* 9 March 2005.

Skipper, John. "Park Inn planning begins." *Mason City Globe Gazette.* 12 March 2005.

Skipper, John. "Group prepares Park Inn proposal." *Mason City Globe Gazette.* 29 March 2005.

Skipper, John. "Bang elected president of Wright hotel group." *Mason City Globe Gazette.* 12 May 2005.

Skipper, John. "Park Inn project receives grant." *Mason City Globe Gazette.* 26 July 2005.

Crawford, Erin. "Making hotel Wright again." *Des Moines Register.* n.d.

"Park Inn project gets $20,500 preservation grant." *Mason City Globe Gazette.* 26 March 2006.

Skipper, John. "Restorers will buy, renovate Wright's bank." *Mason City Globe Gazette.* 1 April 2006.

Skipper, John. "We're Great!" *Mason City Globe Gazette.* 28 October 2006.

Secondary Sources

"A Brief History of the City National Bank of Mason City, Iowa." *Western Architect* 27:12, December 1911.

Advertisement for the Park Inn Coffee Shop, n.d. Vertical file "Park Inn Hotel Archival Material," Bergland and Gram Architects, Mason City, Iowa.

Advertisement. *Mason City Globe Gazette.* "Formal Opening of the newly remodeled Park Inn Lounge Café for Friday, June 18, C.I. Ellingson, Prop. (n.d.)

"Arizona Biltmore Resort and Spa." 10 July 2009. <http://www.arizonaguide.com/DisplayListing.aspx?id=5296>.

AT&T Learning Network. "About Us." 2006. <www.saveamericastreatures.org> (1 June 2007).

Bergland and Cram Architects, Mason City, Iowa.

Cre-8-ing. "Prairie School in Mason City." 2005. <www.stockmanhouse.org> (5 June 2007).

Dyton Creative, 2007, "News," 22 May 2007 <http://www.wrightonthepark. org>.

Fields, Jeanette. "Bock to the Future." *Journal*, n.d. Article reproduced in *Prairie School Vol. II.* Lee P. Loomis Archives, Mason City, Iowa.

"First National Bank of Dwight," brochure. Wright on the Park Inc. office, Mason City, Iowa.

Frank Lloyd Wright Foundation. Scottsdale, AZ.

Frank Lloyd Wright Monograph. 1907-1913. A.D.A. EDITA, Tokyo, 1987.

"Frank Lloyd Wright: Midway Gardens. 11 July 2009. <http://www.planetclaire.org/flw/Mg.html>.

"Frank Lloyd Wright's Wasmuth Portfolio." Exhibition Archive. *ArchiTech.* 9 September 2009. <http://www.architechgallery.com>.

Gill, Brendon. *Many Masks: A Life of Frank Lloyd Wright.* New York: Ballantine Books, 1987.

History of Franklin and Cerro Gordo County. Springfield, IL: Union Publishing Co., 1883.

"Imperial Hotel: 1912-1923." 11 July 2009. <http://ww,obs,irg.fkw.byukdubgs.Unoeruak?Imperial.htm>.

Kaler, Howard. "Park Inn Hotel Operating Criteria." May 2006. Wright on the Park Office, Mason City, Iowa.

KSMN Information. Vertical file, "The Communicator." Lee P. Loomis Archives, Mason City, Iowa.

Lipman, Jon. Past President, Frank Lloyd Wright Building Conservancy. Speech to Mason City City Council. 3 March 1999.

MacGregor, Ann. Wright on the Park, Inc. Executive Director. Mason City, Iowa.

Manson, Grant Carpenter. *Frank Lloyd Wright to 1910: The First Golden Age.* New York: Reinhold Publishing 1958.

"Mason City, Iowa: An Architectural Heritage." *Inventory of Historic and Architecturally Significant Buildings.* 1971. *Prairie School, Vol. I.* Lee P. Loomis Archives. Mason City Public Library, Mason City, Iowa.

"Mason City bond issue passes." Radio Iowa. 7 Nov. 2007. 23 July 2009. <http://www.radioiowa.com/datesearch/index/cfm?searchterm=11%2FO7%2F2007>.

McCoy, Robert. "Rock Crest/Rock Glen Prairie Planning in Iowa." *The Prairie School Review*, 5,3 (1968): 9.

McCoy, Robert. Telephone interview, 4 June 2007, Mason City, Iowa.

McCoy, Robert. "Mason City Walking Tour Guide." Mason City, Iowa: Larson Printing, 2003.

"Modern Architecture." *Absolute Astronomy.com: Exploring the universe of knowledge.* 10 July 2009. <http://www.absoluteastronomy.com/topics/ Modern_architecture>.

National Register Application, "Description." Vertical file, "National Register Applic. 1972," Wright on the Park office, Mason City, Iowa.

Officer, Lawrence and Samuel Williamson. "Relative Value in U.S. Dollars." 2007. <http://measuringworth.com> (19 June 2007).

Osgood, Sue. "Bauhaus defined." *Helium,* 10 July 2009. <http:www.helium.com/items/1248880-baushaus-defined>.

Sage, Leland. *A History of Iowa.* Ames: Iowa State University Press, 1974.

Scully, Vincent. *Modern Architecture: The Architecture of Democracy.* New York: George Braziller, 1961.

State of Iowa: Governors Office: Board Profile: Vision Iowa Board. 23 July 2009. <http://openup,iowa.gov/board/Vision+Iowa+Board/140>.

Storrer, William Allin. *FL^LW Update.* 10 July 2009. <http://www.franklloydwrightinfo.comdamietta.html>.

Storrer, William Allin. *The Frank Lloyd Wright Companion.* Chicago and London: Oxford University Press, 1993.

Walsh, Margaret. *Making Connections.* Burlington, VT: Ashgate Publishing Company, 2000.

Wheeler, J.H. *History of Cerro Gordo County, Iowa. Vol. II.* Chicago: Lewis Publishing Co. 1910.

Who's Who in Mason City Iowa, local publication, 1929, Lee P. Loomis Archives, Mason City Public Library, Mason City, Iowa.

"William Drummond." 11 July 2009. <http://www.prairiestyles.com/drummond.htm>.

Wilson, Richard and Sidney Robinson. *The Prairie School in Iowa.* Ames: Iowa State University Press, 1977.

Wright, Frank Lloyd. *Buildings Plans and Designs.* New York: Horizon Press Publishers, 1957.

Wright on the Park, Inc., Mason City, Iowa.

"Wright's Illinois Work." 13 August 2009. <http://www.dgunning.org/architecture/Illinois/willits.htm>.

Wright, Walter Burton, Photograph Collection. Lee P. Loomis Archives, Mason City Public Library, Mason City, Iowa.

Index

Afterword by Dr. Robert McCoy

Dr. McCoy, retired orthopedic surgeon, hon. AIA, past member of the board of the Frank Lloyd Wright Building Conservancy, current board member of the Walter Burley Griffin Society, author of articles on the buildings and member of Wright on the Park's Board of Directors, has been involved from the beginning in the effort to preserve not just The Historic Park Inn Hotel and City National Bank, but the Stockman House and the homes in the Rock Crest/Rock Glenn area as well. He and his wife Bonnie own and live in a 1913 Walter Burley Griffin Prairie Style home and made the significant contribution of the Wright-designed art-glass ceiling panels found there. His on-going commitment and involvement give him a unique perspective on this project.

For a town of 28,000 at the beginning of the twenty-first century, an undertaking of this magnitude would, to any sane individual, have seemed impossible. When those of us with a clear idea of the building's significance also had a clear idea of the price tag, the sum of nearly $20,000,000 made it even more daunting.

By the 1870's, Mason City had become a railroad center, and manufacturing and the entrepreneurial spirit boomed. Things were still on the upswing in 1908 when Blythe and Markley saw no limits to the city they were helping to build. They turned to a rising young architect whose reputation had not yet reached Mason City's general public. Wright's proposal excited their imaginations and feelings of self-worth. When the City National Bank and Hotel was completed in 1910, the people felt something big and completely up-to-date had been achieved. Within a year, a competitor would build an eight-story bank and office building across the corner. A decade later, the movers and shakers felt a 43-room hotel was not big enough to meet the increasing needs of the city. They feared its small size was costing them business. The same banker, manufacturer, competitor became the chief investor and driving force behind the construction of an eight-story, 250-room hotel with all the accouterments of a town many times Mason City's size. Then came the banking crisis of the 1920s when four out of five of the town's banks failed. Before the architectural world had noticed it, the bank was sold to a developer who remodeled it into multiple businesses and changed its appearance and, worse, its pleasing proportions.

At the same time, the Park Inn Hotel began a long, slow decline. Life-long Mason City residents who had known the building all their lives would no longer recommend it to friends. Foreclosures haunted its owners

and an undercapitalized venture to turn it into rental apartments and retail space predictably failed. Another developer took over and remodeled its first floor for businesses, but the upper floors were increasingly home to ever-greater numbers of pigeons. The developer won one of the highest REAP restoration grants given in Iowa for that year, but it was never matched or utilized for the hotel's restoration. A new, well-capitalized plan emerged from Heartland Properties of Madison, Wisconsin, proposing to rehabilitate the building to affordable housing. The city council rejected the plan in 1999 and persuaded the Mason City Foundation to take on the restoration.

Although the foundation took major steps in the project, the biting-criticism it faced for not having accomplished the restoration in the five allotted years forced it to turn the hotel back to the city. In this milieu of futility and discouragement in January, 2005, the city council both advertised unsuccessfully for a developer on eBay and asked for a citizens' group to form, come forward, and develop this heretofore thankless and unsuccessful task. By March of that year, Wright on the Park, Inc. did organize, come forward and gain acceptance by the council, giving you the story you have just been reading.

At this juncture, the financing is in place. . . contracts have been awarded . . . and the major construction has started. After construction is finished, the important chapter that will make this story complete begins. It will be a long chapter as visitors from our state, our country and the world come to experience first hand the designing skill of Frank Lloyd Wright, America's greatest architect of the twentieth century, by staying in his building for a few days and experiencing in its spaces the genius of Wright's work

Dr. Robert and Bonnie McCoy outside their home in Mason City. The house was designed in the Prairie Style by Walter Burley Griffin in 1913.